A Season of Night

A Season of Night

New Orleans Life after Katrina

IAN McNULTY

University Press of Mississippi

JACKSON

www.upress.state.ms.us

The University Press of Mississippi is a member of the Association of American University Presses.

Lyric excerpt on page 77: From "Romance in the Dark" from the Paramount Picture *Romance in the Dark*. Words and Music by Sam Coslow and Gertrude Niesen. Copyright © 1938 (Renewed 1967) by Paramount Music Corporation. International Copyright Secured. All Rights Reserved.

First printing 2008
∞

Library of Congress Cataloging-in-Publication Data

McNulty, Ian, 1973–
    A season of night : New Orleans life after Katrina / Ian McNulty.
        p.   cm.
    ISBN 978-1-934110-91-1 (alk. paper)
    1. New Orleans (La.)—Description and travel. 2. New Orleans (La.)—Social life and customs—21st century. 3. City and town life—Louisiana—New Orleans. 4. Street life—Louisiana—New Orleans. 5. New Orleans (La.)—Social conditions—21st century. 6. Hurricane Katrina, 2005. 7. McNulty, Ian, 1973– 8. New Orleans (La.)—Biography. I. Title.
    F379.N54M39 2008
    976.3'35064—dc22

                                                                            2007043571

British Library Cataloging-in-Publication Data available

For my mother, Mary Jane Quadrini,
and my father, Wild Bill McNulty

Contents

A Season of Night

One Rowed Home

I fled my New Orleans home in a car speeding up the old River Road the day before Hurricane Katrina struck. I crept back to it two weeks later in a boat, drifting slowly through the ruined urban wilderness of brown floodwater and battered houses that had been my neighborhood.

We floated up to Canal Street on the wrong side of the frontier separating the empty, dry wards of the evacuated city from the empty, flooded ones. Military helicopters hammered away overhead, whole black flights of them in formation or individual machines flying low with crewmen framed in their open doors, scanning the wretched blocks below. Occasionally, a fan boat roared down the wide city boulevard. These are the type of shallow-draft watercraft built to carry hunters through Cajun swamplands, though now they were bearing armed posses. Their low decks were crammed with guys dressed in a full catalogue of law enforcement uniforms and toting M-16s or combat shotguns, wearing mirrored sunglasses and flak jackets strapped over sweat-soaked T-shirts. They streaked through flooded traffic intersections, skimming this way to dodge the dinosaur limbs of felled oak trees languishing in the water, cutting that way past a reef of car roofs and truck cabs lined up in their submerged parking spots.

The desperate rescue work of lifting people off rooftops and embarking them from their porches and balconies was over. The thousands of people trapped at the Superdome and convention center or stranded on the blistering highways were all gone, trucked out to other stadiums and churches and convention centers around the region. The fires that had clouded the skyline were mostly out. The thugs and looters who had rampaged across the city were gone or subdued, finally outgunned and hiding out or simply funneled into the crowds of exhausted people pressed into buses and airliners and dispersed across the country.

About all that remained was the water, a vast city street grid of channels and canals lined with ruined homes and businesses and patrolled over by the helicopters and swamp boats. We watched a fan boat cruise by as we idled in the shadow of a flooded church, basically hiding until it passed. We were doing nothing wrong, but the mood over the city was tense. The boatloads of armed men radiated the don't-fuck-with-us vibe even from a good distance away. The grip of order imposed on this suddenly wild, broken place seemed tenuous, something achieved with firepower and mass evacuations. There was no telling where anyone really stood. The deputies and the game wardens and the soldiers looked strange gunning down the flooded streets. But I knew I would look strange to them too, floating along in a small, commandeered craft with a skinny man and a nervous woman, the three of us slowly moving into a neighborhood from which people had been fighting with tears and frantic effort to escape just a few days prior.

The skinny man was Keith O'Brien, a news reporter and a close friend, and the nervous woman was a news photographer we had met an hour earlier. Our boat was a little flat-bottom skiff we had found abandoned a few blocks away, where a ridge of land above the flood level had served as a grassy landing pad for helicopters for a while during the evacuation. We were in the Mid-City neighborhood in the heart of New Orleans and we were heading for my house.

We advanced at the most incrementally slow pace, moving a meter or so at a time as we negotiated tangles of branches and countless snares concealed under the brown water. The plodding pace allowed us to take in with slack-jawed wonder the surreal landscape—the pickup trucks with bathtub rings of grime leading laterally down their sides to the water line, the oak trees rising up from streets that now looked like long, straight swamp passes, the houses with boarded-up windows or kicked-in doors, the horrific sound of dogs howling and moaning from unseen windows after two sweltering, abandoned weeks.

This was homecoming, a moment for which I had wished and schemed practically since the storm hit. The disaster was over and the recovery had yet to begin. The city's odds and future were being determined elsewhere—in Washington, in Baton Rouge, in offices and conference rooms and wherever New Orleans people had found refuge to try to sort out their displaced lives. But New Orleans itself was under the pall of trauma. It was a flooded city without life, the skeleton crew of its population made up entirely of military people, media people, and the few remaining residents hiding or negotiating to resist evacuation like cornered stowaways. Everything looked doomed, and somewhere along the way as we floated through Mid-City in our little boat I decided I wanted to return for good as soon as possible.

Two weeks earlier, Hurricane Katrina was just the latest in a long line of storms to menace the gulf, and our city was complete in all its glorious, troubled, storied, simmering ways. I had lived in New Orleans for six years by then, and it turns out those had been six quiet years for hurricanes. People talked with reverence about the killer storms, Betsy in 1965 or Camille in 1969, and whenever a hurricane looked like it might head toward Louisiana there was quickened talk about the Big One—the storm that could come straight up the river, swamp the levees, and inundate New Orleans. But it was still all a little hard to grasp. The Big One was a threat so terrible and unstoppable that a lot of us regarded it in mythological terms, like the prospect of the moon dropping through the sky to crush Australia.

When a storm reared up, I took the same hurricane precautions I saw other people taking around me. But it really didn't have much sense of gravity. One year, my friend Rene and I cut sheets of plywood to fit over my windows in advance of a storm that looked bad at first but showed up in New Orleans only as overtime weather coverage. Many people evacuated the city for that storm, but we stayed at my place, and, when we heard the storm would hit elsewhere and that we were safe, we went outside with buckets of house paint and decorated the plywood over the windows. We reasoned that we would need to use them again for another hurricane at some point and felt we should at least make them colorful. On the boards over the first-floor windows we painted a smile with bulbous lips and a bushy mustache, and on the boards over the smaller attic windows above we painted happy, lolling eyeballs. From the street, it looked like the house had a big, stoned, grinning face, and everyone who saw it laughed and eventually agreed the face looked a lot like Rene's. So, that year, my most ambitious hurricane preparation devolved into an art project.

Officials often urged people to evacuate during hurricane scares, but again I always based my decisions on whatever my New Orleans–bred friends planned to do. These were guys who had grown up interpreting the TV weatherman's hurricane warnings as advertisements for at least one day out of school, and maybe more if the storm made landfall nearby and happened to do some damage to the local utility network. They never left during a hurricane scare in the years I had lived in the city, and neither did I. Two days before Katrina, on Saturday, August 27, 2005, everyone was taking it easy.

But when I got around to calling people the next morning, my friends were already on the road, stuck in traffic and freaking out. The storm had made its fatal turn during the night, and it suddenly looked very much like the Big One. I took stock of my nearly bare bachelor's cupboards, my lean supply of bottled water, my complete lack of preparation for myself or my dog—a plump yellow Labrador named the Amazing Dr. Watson—and I quickly decided to leave. I secured the comically painted plywood over the front windows of my house and packed an overnight bag, a move that later proved rather meager but at the time seemed completely rational. Sure, there was a potentially killer storm en route and at least in theory I understood that I was fleeing for my life, but I was sure we really would be returning in a day or two, just like all the city's other close calls when my friends had enjoyed free days off from school.

I loaded Dr. Watson into my beat-up old Cadillac—a dented, beautiful, rusted, 1971-model sedan with leaks and laughable gas mileage and what I regard as real style—and we set off for the relative safety of Baton Rouge, where my friend Kathleen Lousteau had offered emergency lodging. I was not even sure my rumbling old heap could make it eighty miles north under normal traffic conditions, never mind when the blazing highway was packed with fleeing families. Friends had already called in with the dread news that they were still within city limits after two hours in their cars. But I took a chance on the River Road, the largely forgotten, prehighway connection to Baton Rouge that winds along the serpentine course of the Mississippi River. All the twists and turns add up to many more miles than the same trip on the interstate, but there was hardly anyone else using it even during the huge evacuation. The dog and I slid past an alternating landscape of old plantation houses, cottages with rusted tin roofs, and gigantic oil refineries by the riverside, and, as the radio gave increasingly calamitous predictions of Katrina's size and strength, we made it to Baton Rouge and Kathleen's house on just one tank of gas.

O'Brien arrived a few days later, after we learned that the levees had failed and when the agony of New Orleans was at its height. He was a New Orleans friend who had moved to Boston just a few months before the storm. He worked as a freelance writer there covering everything from neighborhood news to science industry issues, but, when the storm hit, there was probably no journalist in New England with a better block-by-block knowledge of New Orleans than O'Brien. Never mind that while living in the city he could get lost and fly into a panic just by straying a few blocks off familiar main drags like Magazine Street or Claiborne Avenue or Elysian Fields. He still knew where those main drags were, and that was much better in terms of crisis reporting from the scene than anyone else from out of town was bringing to the situation. While the captions of international wire photos would sometimes mistake St. Claude Avenue (remarkable for its neglected homes, weed-choked sidewalks, and burned-out cars) with St. Charles Avenue (remarkable for its postcard-worthy mansions, historic streetcar line, and live oak canopy), O'Brien knew the territory and the people. So the *Boston Globe* hired him and sent him to New Orleans along with a photographer whose previous assignment had been to follow troops fighting the Taliban in the mountains of Afghanistan.

O'Brien's arrival jolted me out of the numb shock that had been gumming up my skull since I learned my city was flooded and being torn apart in unchecked bedlam. The hurricane had enough fury when it passed over Baton Rouge to knock down many trees, one of which simultaneously cut the power to Kathleen's house and blocked our cars in her driveway. So we got most of our early news about the disaster sitting around the kitchen table in her sweltering house and listening to unbelievable radio broadcasts. It unfolded like a story told in pieces rather than something we could see ourselves, even through the proxy of TV. But O'Brien went to New Orleans immediately after he arrived and began feeding us daily firsthand reports in the evenings when he returned. That made this thing suddenly real to me and aroused a fierce desire to get back into the city, even just for a glimpse.

At the time, I was working for Hibernia Bank, which was a big-time bank for Louisiana, a homegrown thing since Reconstruction but small potatoes compared with the large regional and national banks. It was the kind of New Orleans company that was listed on the New York Stock Exchange and had all the normal midtier corporate trappings but also had senior managers who would sneak out for fried oyster po-boys from a downtown diner whenever they could evade a more official luncheon with unpromising banquet food. In the summertime, bankers here still broke out the blue-striped seersucker suits, and whenever the bank hired a brass band to play for a company party even the most buttoned-up among the executive administrative assistants could be relied upon to get down and dance just as though the marble-trimmed lobby was Tipitina's music hall. The bank quickly reorganized its management structure in Baton Rouge on the heels of the storm, and I caught up with my bosses at the capital city's downtown branch where the executives were all but bivouacked in the hallways and offices and lobbies. Some of them, like me, were still wearing the clothes they had evacuated in a few days earlier.

For a displaced New Orleans guy, a paying job with a company that could manage to keep its direct deposit clicking even though its payroll offices were destroyed by the storm was suddenly a very precious thing. But to me the job was also a great frustration. I was working day and night for my little part in stitching the bank back together, while O'Brien was making daily forays into New Orleans during what anyone could see was a monumental time in the old city's history. He would return deeply upset and on the verge of tears, but we were all deeply upset and on the verge of tears. If I had the choice of crying in a borrowed Baton Rouge bank office or crying back in my city and seeing my house and crawling around the bizarre disaster zone and hearing people's stories, I would take the latter.

After a week or so, a growing number of my friends had begun sneaking back into New Orleans. The city was officially closed, blockaded on the highways by the National Guard, but people found ways around that with passes, by calling on friends with pull, or by simple subterfuge. It seemed like a lot of people I knew were visiting their houses in the unflooded neighborhoods, putting tarps over shattered windows, securing doors, getting a tiny bit of peace of mind that the place was still there, and grabbing little niceties like a change of shoes and those insurance documents some of us had neglected to take in our frenzied flight from home. I badly wanted to get in. Finally, two weeks after the storm hit, I got a day off from work and started planning an excursion.

O'Brien and I and another journalist friend from New Orleans, Paul Rioux, came up with the idea of getting ourselves back to town in time for the broadcast of the first New Orleans Saints game after the storm, which fell on Sunday, September 11. If listening to a football game on home turf seemed like a trite goal surrounded by the enormity of loss and fear that was consuming our lives then, there was also a symbolism to it that we couldn't resist, like defiantly running up a flag on the front lawn after a national tragedy. We were going to New Orleans, and I was determined to get to my house in the flood zone, but along the way maybe we could manage a tiny, symbolic dose of that long-gone normalcy from pre-Katrina life. In this case, that meant cheering on the home team in a New Orleans barroom.

We knew the pub Molly's at the Market would be open. It was one of a handful of bars that managed to remain in operation on the high ground of the French Quarter, reopening just a few hours after Katrina had passed and while the flooding and looting were hitting their stride elsewhere. O'Brien had been there on his news reporting visits, and, even though Molly's had no electricity, we were all sure it would have the game playing on a battery-powered radio. Just in case, though, we stopped at a Wal-Mart on the way out of Baton Rouge to buy our own radio and batteries. While we were there, we also decided to buy some supplies to donate to the pub's cause, cut off as it was from power and deliveries but admirably still serving drinks. We filled our rented Jeep with beer, cold cuts, Band-Aids, hand sanitizer, lighters, and as much ice as we could store.

I also picked up a coach's whistle from the sports department and used its lanyard to hang my corporate ID around my neck. O'Brien and Paul Rioux had legit press passes for getting in and out of the city, but I would have to bluff it by flashing my meaningless Hibernia Bank badge to the soldiers at the checkpoints. Virtually everyone who was making it back into New Orleans at that point had some kind of ID on a lanyard, as if the whole city were some job site or movie set that required credentials. We reasoned that my photo and an obscure bank name under a sheen of laminate would seem official enough.

The ruse worked, and, with O'Brien lead-footing the Jeep between checkpoints on the otherwise empty highway, we cruised past the storm-whipped cypress forests separating the two cities and into New Orleans's battered suburbs. We pulled off the interstate, crossed one final checkpoint at the parish line, and were in the city again.

Everything looked pretty good at first. I was ready for Armageddon, for block after block of burned-down buildings and bodies in the street, as we had heard about on the radio. But Uptown New Orleans seemed fine. It was empty and violently pruned, but clearly intact.

As we moved downtown we started seeing people. Virtually all of them looked official in some way, and most were also armed. Men walked around casually with shotguns held against their chests or sidearms riding openly on hip holsters. Uniformed military patrols trooped by with machine guns. From army units to private contractors, everyone was coming to New Orleans as to a war zone. We crossed Canal Street, the historic division between the old French Quarter and the American sector. The wide downtown stretch of the street was now a parking lot of giant, sleek motor coaches, RVs and tractor trailers packed with equipment for the national media, with armed men sauntering everywhere in between.

We drove to Decatur Street and parked in front of Molly's. Jim Monaghan, the bar owner, came outside to the sidewalk as we pulled up. His eyes were dark and heavy-lidded, his bearing fatigued. If he had gotten any sleep since the storm, it didn't show. A couple of liberally tattooed men followed him outside, like midshipmen backing up their skipper, and they looked us over as we prepared to show off the bounty we had delivered from Wal-Mart for their benefit.

"We got beer," O'Brien announced. "We got food. We got"—he paused for a dramatic beat—"ice!"

"Great," Jim said, sounding sincere but exhausted.

"Where do you want the ice?" Paul asked.

"Oh, ah, fellas." Jim motioned to the other men behind him. "Put these bags in the back with the rest, please."

"The rest?" I asked. "You have ice?"

"Oh yeah, well, we get pretty regular deliveries. Every news guy in town right now brings us ice and beer. I guess they want to make sure they can get a cold beer somewhere."

Sure enough, our contribution was just another brick in the wall of provisions Molly's had amassed. We walked into the bar with our stuff and dumped the beers in the bin of the powerless but already brimful ice machine. There was a veritable sandwich board of cold cuts and white bread on a table in the corner. The bar looked fully stocked with liquor.

The wide French doors at the front of the pub were open, but the sunlight penetrated only a few feet, leaving most of the place in shadow. There were four or five people in the bar, most of them just hanging around, drinking cans of Coke. It was dead quiet. A young guy sitting close to the door was carefully examining a porno magazine by the sunlight falling on the bar, turning over each page delicately as if inspecting a catalogue for an expensive purchase.

"You'll get hairy palms," Jim told him in deadpan. Then he served Paul Rioux and me two of the beers we had just brought in and poured O'Brien a gin and tonic. "You want a lime in that?" he asked. "Someone brought us limes yesterday."

The Saints game might have been the organizing principle for the trip, but, after cheering to the little corner radio for a few plays, we all grew more interested in getting out to the city around us. Paul Rioux went off to do some reporting from Chalmette, and O'Brien and I set out to find a way to my house, picking up a new *Boston Globe* photographer along the way. The plan, for lack of a better word, was to drive around the edge of the flood zone and try to find an abandoned boat we could take from there.

When we got back in the Jeep, the trip around the city quickly became a rush of frantic movement. New Orleans may have been under de facto martial law, but no laws or rules at all seemed to concern the few drivers on the storm-wracked streets, ourselves included. Many streets were blocked by heavy equipment, trailers, or piles of storm debris, and any street that was clear became a free-for-all. One-way street designations were out the window through the tight grid of the Central Business District. We swerved around water-filled craters in the middle of streets, the abandoned police barricades here and there, and the mounds of fallen bricks from century-old buildings crumbled in the storm or subsequent fires. We flew through intersections and careened around wreckage and street corners on our way to the edge of Mid-City.

We tried a few routes into the flood zone, but everywhere the water grew too deep before we could find any sign of boats. We traced the crescent of dry land back through downtown again, sweating copiously in the heat of the day and punching through block after block fast. We passed the French Quarter and headed up Esplanade Avenue to the end of Bayou St. John, an old urban waterway and the spot where the floodwater began again in earnest. Our luck swung around completely here, and we found boats of every description for the taking on the yellowed grassy banks of the bayou, marooned there as the floodwater began its slow recession back from the brink. There were canoes and flat-bottom skiffs painted in camouflage hunting schemes, but also sizeable cabin cruisers and small fishing boats, plus a great variety of washed-up industrial debris and household items ditched there as people fled.

The crowning glory of it all, though, was a destroyed helicopter lying on its side on the grass by the bayou. I had heard a news report about a helicopter crashing in the area near my house after the storm, and this must have been it. The crew had reportedly walked away unhurt, but the machine still looked impressively shattered. Its tail was crumpled, and its rotor blades had snapped off after gouging deep troughs in the ground around it. It was as gruesomely captivating as a dead whale beached on the shore.

Before the storm, I had taken my dog jogging on this same stretch of bayou where we stood now with gaping mouths and unbelieving eyes. Friends gathered here on New Year's Eve to watch fireworks and drink cheap champagne, and on cool afternoons there would be picnics all around while kids learned to fish along the slim, meandering bayou's edge. Now the area looked like a recently contested battlefield with its helicopter carcass and washed-up Dunkirk flotilla. There were even a few dead fish drying up in the sun where the retreating floodwaters had left them.

We grabbed the nearest boat and launched it at the water's edge. As soon as I climbed in, water began to gush from a hole that would have taken a wine cork to plug. I hopped out, getting only slightly wet, and we tried again with the next closest boat. This one proved seaworthy. We found a broomstick and some thick palm fronds on the ground that we could use to propel the craft, and O'Brien and the photographer slipped into the thick rubber waders they had brought along.

We set out down flooded Jefferson Davis Parkway, passing the ominous hulk of a community hospital, the column rows of live oak trees with torn-out limbs, the snapped light posts, the dangling power lines, and the roofs of sunken cars. Our slow, sloshing progress sent ripples over the still water toward the doors of my neighborhood's houses. It was too familiar and too weird all at once, and I responded by mouthing an inchoate stream of cussing that I remember as being remarkable even by the high standards for outraged vulgarity of the time.

"I know, man," O'Brien counseled me. "I know."

My curses were starting to take on at least coherent form as we approached the major roadway intersection at Canal Street. On one corner was a Methodist church, a large, sturdy, conservative-looking brick building. The cross atop its tall steeple was bent severely on its side as if it had been hit by something heavy way up there. Back down on the street, the church had one of those letter board signs outside where inspirational messages were posted for passing motorists. There was a tangle of broken oak limbs around it now, and it was streaked by black stains from the higher floodwater, but the lettering was still intact and rose just above the current water level to show its prestorm message, which read, "There is a dawn in every darkness."

The photographer snapped pictures, and we huddled there a while, floating in the shadow of the church, as one of the fan boats full of armed law enforcement types buzzed past on the other side of Canal Street.

We were getting closer to my house, but first O'Brien and the photographer had to visit a specific block of the neighborhood for their stories. They wanted to document one defined area from flood through whatever the months ahead would bring. We picked a stretch that had Finn McCool's Irish pub on one corner, a plumbing supply house at the other, and, in between, the homes of a diverse mix of single people, young couples, gay guys, black people, white people, and retired people. It was a good slice of New Orleans diversity that was now also flooded and deserted. We paddled from building to building as O'Brien and the photographer inspected houses and took pictures and notes. I sat in the boat on the verge of panic, as tense as a bathwater soap bubble trying not to burst, convinced that we would be taken for looters and shot at by antsy deputies.

But at last we started to my house. We had been in the water for a while now, and the photographer was getting cranky about it. There was also the looming curfew to consider. We had to be gone or hidden by 6 p.m. But I didn't care about any of that. My house was only two blocks away and we were going there.

Every foot we traveled through that water was achingly slow, like trying to wade through sand. The closer we got, the more familiar but disjointed everything looked. The houses all had sunlight reflecting back up from the water in shimmering patterns on their walls and porch ceilings, like the kind of undulating light play you see on the hulls of boats riding gently at mooring. Some of the big neighborhood trees had been snapped in half, and one had dramatically torn the entire rear wall off a two-story Victorian house, which stood with its bedrooms exposed in the manner of a life-size dollhouse. Looking up at it from the water, we could see the beds and their sheets, the lamps and the dresser with clothes still sticking out of its drawers.

We turned the corner and entered my block of South Scott Street. I knew every single house on the block and everyone who lived in each one. There was hardly a sound besides the distant cries of another trapped, starving dog. The pallid water stretched out before the bow of the boat and down my street for as far as I could see. The houses here are all raised up at least a few feet above the ground, and I noticed immediately that none of them was still flooded. Weatherboards were stained with horizontal black lines about a foot above the porches, but the water had clearly come down since that high point. My clenched heart opened with hope as we neared my house.

But my calculations of water depth ended with a bolt of fear as we passed Miss Anne's house. Miss Anne had lived on my block forever and she lived alone. She was fiercely independent. She had a gold-painted 1973 Cutlass coupe that she drove to the grocery store three blocks away and to the beauty parlor a few blocks past that. Whenever it rained, she went outside with a plastic rain cap over her hair to cover the car's leaky windshield with a tarp. It was her prized possession. As we floated by in the boat, I saw the half-submerged Cutlass parked in front of her porch. I pictured Miss Anne. If the car had stayed behind, she probably had too. I pictured her dead on the moldy floor.

"Miss Anne!" I cried out. Then, to O'Brien and the startled photographer: "My neighbor. That's her car. She might be in there. Old lady. Miss Anne!"

We all started calling her name up at her silent house. I poled over to her porch with the broomstick, but the Cutlass blocked my way. O'Brien waded around and pushed on the front door. It hadn't been locked or even latched and opened without effort. "I don't smell anything dead," he said encouragingly before ducking inside. He came back outside after a minute and announced there was no one inside.

We kept going. My house was just three doors down, and in a minute I was floating right up to my front steps as if to a marina pier. I disembarked carefully from the skiff and stepped onto my muddy porch. My hands were shaking a bit, but with some concentration I made them fish the house keys out of my jeans.

"Here goes," I said over my shoulder to O'Brien, trying to sound nonchalant for some reason.

I pushed the door open, feeling a little like an archeologist on the brink of a buried Egyptian cell. But there were no old bones here—just my living room, and it looked a lot like I had left it. The couches were wet and there was gunk on the floors, but the place had drained out. The paintings and photos were still on the walls. Bottles of booze clanged together a bit on the rickety bar when I walked past it. The candles and bits of costumes and other doodads I had set up altar-like on my mantelpiece were all where I had left them.

The place smelled, but more like the mildew of moist neglect than the reek of moldy flood. I trotted through the house. I was on a mission to grab a few things, but I was incredibly disconcerted, almost dizzy. I was aware of my feet on the floor, of my hands touching doorknobs. I felt like I was watching myself move through a dreamscape. Still, it was clear even then that I could repair this place. It still felt like home.

O'Brien and the photographer were waiting outside in the water, and the afternoon was drawing closer to curfew. There was no time to do anything useful to the house besides open a few windows for venting. I stomped upstairs to my bedroom and grabbed a pair of dress shoes, which somehow seemed important at the time. I riffled through drawers frantically to lay my hands on insurance papers. Passing my little bar on the way back outside, I grabbed a bottle of champagne I had put away a few months before the storm for some special occasion. This, I figured, had to qualify.

Two From Pillar to Post

Back in Baton Rouge, time passed like the days on someone else's calendar, quick and meaningless. There was much work and worry, but most of all each day just marked off time until I could manage another trip back to New Orleans.

The work at the bank continued at a furious pace as we tried to shift operations to other sites and find scattered employees and re-assure frantic customers. O'Brien continued his daily trips back to the city and fed us reports. The floodwater had been drained out of Mid-City just a few days after we boated through my neighbor-hood, and one afternoon O'Brien sent a text message to say he was driving down my dried-out street and past my house.

It was killing me. If I was with him, I could be in my house. I could be trying to salvage flooded belongings or at least taking stock of how things stood in my neighborhood. I was stuck in Baton Rouge, earning money I was desperate to have, but stuck nonethe-less. Everyone I knew from New Orleans was stuck somewhere else, searching for glimpses of the city we recognized on TV or Web sites, trying to piece together some kind of plan on secondhand re-connaissance and make some sense of all the conflicting predic-tions from officialdom. Distance made me feel helpless and irrele-vant to what was happening in my city, even if all that was actually happening was the slow, silent retreat of floodwater and the rapid bloom of mold and reek. So when the bank managers gave us an-other weekend off, I knew I had to make another run back home.

In the morning, I topped off the car with gas, bought canned food and cleaning supplies, loaded Dr. Watson into the back seat, and hit the road. Once again, the highway was empty, and I had the interstate to myself as I drove as fast as my old car could manage. I had my bank ID badge ready as I pulled off the highway near New Orleans, but this time the combat-armed National Guardsmen just gave a casual wave as the car bounced over the parish border and into the city.

The streets were impassable at some points, but after an improvised and circuitous route around the side streets I was back in Mid-City and driving along the same blocks I had floated over with O'Brien two weeks before. I parked in front of my house and let the dog out. Dr. Watson sniffed the air, and I took a big look around. Somehow, the place looked worse drained than it had flooded. The water, at least, had covered up all the damage and debris. With the novelty of floating along my block now gone, I could more fully appreciate the true extent of the devastation. Everything was crusted over with a strange residue. The pavement and even the dead grass crackled as my shoes and the dog's paws padded over it. Miss Anne's flooded old Cutlass was just down the street, its vintage gold paint job clouded now, and there were plenty of other cars left flooded and destroyed along the block.

Inside my house, I began to lay a more detailed and realistic inventory of damage over my first rushed, happy assessment of the place from the flood visit. Everything on the first floor would have to go. All the kitchen stuff was ruined. Mold was blooming here and there on the walls. Amazingly, the floors still appeared fine, the century-old boards unbuckled and still tight. The electrical system was cooked, as were the AC and the water heaters in the shed out back. Upstairs, a number of windows I hadn't boarded up were broken, but the rooms still looked more or less intact.

I went back outside and looked up and down the empty, shattered block. Occasionally a pickup truck rumbled down a side street a block or two away. These were the first of the rebuilding crews, and most of them were newly arrived Latino men. They crammed in eight or ten to a truck and drove to whatever address the owner had hired them to gut sight unseen.

I had one errand ahead of me before I could get into my first pass at debris hauling and cleaning. Via text message from Baton Rouge, I had promised to make a supply run to my friend Todd Windisch, who was living back in his apartment about a mile away from my house. Todd was a building contractor and had a pass to get back into town and get to work. He basically smuggled his wife, Erin Peacock, through the checkpoints without a pass by telling the soldiers at the parish line that she was a stripper and had been called in to entertain the troops at a Bourbon Street club. In reality, Erin was an office administrator for a health care company, but Todd's story impressed the soldiers, who waved them through with big smiles.

Todd had been text messaging back and forth with his displaced friends scattered across the country and running all over town to their houses and businesses to put plywood over missing windows, nail their kicked-in doors shut again, and check on roofs. He was essentially giving emergency first aid to buildings before their owners could make it back, and I figured anyone performing such noble service deserved a care package from the well-stocked grocery store shelves of Baton Rouge. So I had a cooler in the back of the car for him loaded with fresh produce, Diet Coke, Italian meats, bread, beer, and ice. I found Todd on the roof of his landlord's apartment building, using a torch to melt a tar roof back on the badly damaged property, while Erin sat downstairs devising homemade fly traps against the sudden and vicious swarms that besieged everyone who ventured into the damp, stinking neighborhoods.

Back at home, I spent the rest of the day hauling out the contents of my flooded rooms and working bleach into the floor and the baseboard molding and everything else that had been covered in water. I called it quits later in the afternoon and took a cold shower. There were no lights and no gas for hot water, and it seemed a bit incredible that the plumbing still worked. I was just overjoyed to find myself standing in my own tub, in my own house, doing something as mundane as showering back in a place that a few weeks earlier I was unsure I would ever see again. I dried off with the same towel I had left on the hook the Saturday before Katrina hit and dressed in my bedroom with a pleasant breeze licking over the jagged glass of the room's broken window. O'Brien was in town again, and he came around at sunset to find me in the house with wet hair and a hyperactive heart. Not only was I back in my house—damaged but intact and still my house—but we had a social agenda to see after.

Just before the storm hit, some friends had opened an ambitious new business called the Savvy Gourmet, a cooking school and kitchen store for well-to-do Uptown foodies. The building made it through the storm fine, but no one back in New Orleans was at all interested in enrolling for classes on cooking with garden herbs or the benefits of braising. Still, the owners picked up the early whiff of opportunity floating in the air just above the fog of despondency. While the city was still drying out, they turned their gleaming new teaching kitchen into a commissary for quick take-out meals. There was hardly anywhere in the city to find hot meals besides the emergency kitchens and Red Cross stations, so the Uptown people who were back flocked to the place.

The Savvy Gourmet also hosted what its owners dubbed "de-vacuation parties," which served as welcome-home events for anyone who wanted to stop by their big and mostly empty retail space. People brought their own beer or wine, sometimes raiding once-sacrosanct collections for precious bottles that had been left too long in the late summer heat without air conditioning to keep their goodness much longer.

Later on, we went down the street to a bar called Le Bon Temps Roule. Like every other unflooded Uptown bar that managed to open so soon after the storm, the place was packed. This one had live music, provided by the Hot 8 Brass Band, which at the time had only six of its eight members accounted for but still managed to play like at least a dozen. They played loud, blowing the big New Orleans street sound with throaty trombones and belly-deep tuba lines. People were moving and hopping and yelling on the dance floor and were jammed around the bar. The crowd even packed into the tavern kitchen, which was out of action and had no food to sell anyway, and people watched the band there from perches on the inert stoves and sinks.

We stayed late and left happy. O'Brien and I were glowing from the music, the drinks, and the reassuring company of people as we climbed into the car and headed to my house across town. I had only made it to the corner, though, when a group of soldiers emerged from the shadows, maybe eight of them in camouflage and all of them watching us intently as they walked into the street and in front of the bumper. They held assault rifles across their chests, and the nearest one waved us down to stop. Others were methodically scanning up and down the main drag of Magazine Street. It was like they had been lying in ambush outside the bar, which was loud, bright, and filled with people just a few yards away from my idling old car. We could still hear the tuba inside even as the military radios crackled with patrol updates around us. One of the soldiers approached the car window.

"Do you know we have a curfew in effect?" he said.

By this point the curfew for unflooded areas like Uptown was midnight, and we well knew it but scoffed at the idea anyway. The bar was open, the brass band was playing, people were drinking and laughing. So what if it was past midnight? We were all back in New Orleans and celebrating. But now we were outside all of that. We were in my car, and the man confronting me at my car window was holding an assault rifle.

"Curfew starts at midnight and it's 2 a.m. now," the soldier said, sounding more like a cop with a ticket book than a trooper with a patrol of heavily armed men backing him up.

O'Brien and I had brought our half-finished drinks from the bar with us in the car. Driving with open drinks is illegal in New Orleans, just as it is anywhere else, but is nonetheless quite common. And on these virtually empty roads, with one-way street directions universally disregarded, with trucks parked across defunct streetcar tracks and on sidewalks in front of shuttered hotels, and with streets in some parts of the city still actually holding neck-deep floodwater, I gave no more thought to putting a beer in the cup holder than I did putting the key in the ignition.

Our drinks were very much on my mind as the soldier at the car window advised us about the curfew restrictions in force. But after a quick look inside the car to make sure we weren't hauling looted TVs and such, they dismissed us with instructions to head straight home. We did, and as I steered toward Mid-City things grew progressively stranger than even this roadside encounter.

Electricity was being restored very slowly around the city, coming on by sections that seemed to be defined by the boundaries of major streets. As we drove through Uptown, streetlights were lit up and so were the windows of some businesses and a few houses here and there. But as we neared Claiborne Avenue, we could see in the distance ahead where all the electricity was cut off. It was desolate enough as we approached it, with abandoned cars partially blocking the road and the beached rescue boats tilted on their dry keels where the receding water had left them. But there were still streetlights here. Up ahead, where the light ceased, was the mouth of darkness, and we plunged into it as suddenly as if a closet door had been slammed behind us.

This was my first night back in the city since the levees failed, and all the daylight time I had spent in my neighborhood did nothing to prepare me for it. Suddenly, the Uptown bars and civic-minded parties were far away. We had crossed the line back into Mid-City, into the realm of the flood, and a dark curtain of gloom had fallen over everything we could see. I was grateful that O'Brien was sitting in the car next to me. We crossed a small overpass, and on the pavement rushing under the car's headlights we could see messages written in spray paint and intended for passing helicopters at the height of the city's desperation when this elevated ramp was a rare summit above the floodwaters. They were simple pleas like "HELP" and "NEED FOOD" and "SICK BABY" in eight-foot-long letters.

We turned onto a side street, and the view through the windscreen grew darker still. The canopy of surviving oaks covered us, lacing their fingers together to mat the sky above the car and hold back the moonlight. There was not even the hint of a person to be seen along the way—no headlights anywhere and no lights in the hundreds of houses and businesses we passed. We went through a few miles of this and made it back to my street. The blocks here gave no evidence of any of the activity they had seen earlier in the day. The crews working in the neighborhood had split before curfew. My car was the only one around besides the flood-ruined hulks left in front of the empty houses.

We got out of the car and looked up. Over the roof of my house the night sky spread constellations I had never seen before with all the usual lighting down below getting in the way. The night also revealed just how much noise I had taken for granted under normal circumstances in the city. Even when it was "quiet," there was still noise—the neighbor's air conditioning unit, a car driving on the next street over, or just the condenser on a fridge turning over in the night downstairs. But with all of this gone, the silence was truly startling. There was just nothing for our ears to register, nothing on which we could set a standard. As I walked up the stairs to my darkened house, I knew my footfalls on the steps were the loudest sound being made for blocks around.

O'Brien and I lit candles inside the house, poured wine into plastic cups, and took the Amazing Dr. Watson for a walk through this once-familiar, now-surreal scene. The silence was all around us and impossible to ignore. It filled the space between us as we walked, and it filled our ears and our mouths as we tried to talk to each other. We instinctively spoke in whispers so as not to challenge the silence. We didn't have much to say anyway, mostly just whispered exclamations and breathy, unbelieving curses. Eventually, I noticed the sound of the dog's metal nametag clinking against the chain of his collar. It seemed so sharp, ringing out through the ghostly street like a small bell tolling as we walked. We continued to Canal Street, which should have been humming with cars and trucks even at this hour on a New Orleans Saturday night but was now as empty as the silent houses and churches and stores that lined it.

"Well, I need to pee," I announced and did so in the middle of the street. It was so dark that I could barely make out O'Brien's form a few feet away, but I heard him doing the same. The neighborhood was so weird, so distorted, that even marking the street like an animal seemed a reasonable thing to do. It almost seemed like an act of pride, like a declaration of our presence in this otherwise lifeless expanse of destruction. Dr. Watson sniffed around at our puddles on the street, looked up at us in the darkness, and wagged his tail furiously.

The next morning I woke up in my own bed with Dr. Watson curled on the floor beside a pile of bleached-stained work clothes. The silence of the night was gone, and noise was back early. Chainsaws were cutting into dead trees and diesel trucks were chugging off with loads of destroyed furniture.

O'Brien was back to work hunting down stories. I had a day of cleaning and scrubbing and demolition ahead of me before I would head back to Baton Rouge. I moved more furniture and boxes of stuff to the street and continued spraying bleach over my house. The fridge had to be ejected. It had seemed empty enough before I evacuated, but now was somehow filled with an unholy stench, and its electrical circuits had anyway been flooded. I found a skateboard in a pile of debris outside and used it as a dolly to wheel the leaking thing from the kitchen through the dining room and living room and out to the porch. It teetered there at the edge for a moment on the skateboard before I gave the hulk its fatal shove and launched it from the porch to the ground three feet below. From there I rolled it roughly in a series of boxy, denting thuds to the sidewalk, finding that the release of a little aggression on the ruined appliance was a soothing exercise.

I took the dog outside a little later that day and found Miss Anne stacking the fallen branches of a magnolia tree in front of her house next to mounds of stinking debris near her ruined old Cutlass. Miss Anne had bought her house in 1947 and had lived there by herself for many years before I arrived in the neighborhood. Feeding the cats that roamed the streets here had been something between her hobby and her calling for years. Every day, before the storm, she had set up a collection of saucers on her front porch filled with canned cat food, water, and sometimes even delights like milk and chicken livers.

I thought she hated me when I first moved into the neighborhood. Sometimes the Amazing Dr. Watson wandered off from my porch to visit the much more appetizing buffet on hers, and when he did it usually led to a thunderous confrontation. Miss Anne would stomp over a few minutes after the dog's feast and holler at me from the sidewalk, reminding me in hard terms that poor old women couldn't be expected to feed my dog every night. But after a few months she abruptly dropped the whole issue and reversed course. She decided she loved the dog and would chastise me if I didn't let him bound up to her well-stocked porch for a snack when we walked past her house.

She was the only other person on the block that morning, but I wasn't all that surprised to find her there cleaning up storm debris in her yard. She wasn't the type to wait around for anyone to tell her how or when to do something. She was wearing a neat, striped blouse and slacks and had a kerchief tied around her neck, which was completely normal for her, though a little dressy for someone making an early visit to a flooded New Orleans neighborhood on a sweltering morning. She also had curlers in her raven-black hair, which I had never observed her wearing before. This was the first time I had seen her since the storm, and I asked where she had been.

"Where have I been? Honey, I been from pillar to post. Let me tell you."

And she told me, breathlessly. The following was delivered at machine-gun pace: "I stayed, honey, I stayed for five days. I had to. I had two cats with me. It was okay, the water only came in the house up to my ankles. I been through hurricanes in this house. I been through Betsy. I been through Camille. You just ride it out. Plenty of people rode it out. Them people across the street there rode it out. Leonard next door rode it out with his boyfriend.

"I had plenty of water, plenty of food. I was doing fine upstairs there. After I think it was four days, a boat came by picking people up. Leonard was leaning out his window shouting at me, saying, 'Anne, you got to go. Anne, you got to go. Anne, you got to go.' Just like that for ten minutes. It was so annoying it gave me a headache. But you can't just jump in a boat like that. I had to get my cats together, I had to get my bags, get my purse together. So I told them to go ahead and maybe I'd go the next day. I tell ya, the one thing that did make me want to leave was that I was listening at WWL on my radio. Thank God I had enough batteries still. And they were saying about looters coming through. I tried to lock my front door here, but I couldn't because the door was all swelled up from the water. I couldn't get it closed all the way. So I thought, if I'm upstairs and I hear any footsteps coming up, well, I'm going to be dead.

"So the next day when a girl came by in a canoe I hollered for her to stop. I said, 'Please, just let me bring my cats. I have them all ready to go in these carriers.' And she said, 'Absolutely not. I'm going to bring you down to the Bayou St. John by Mercy Hospital and a helicopter is going to take you out of here.'

"So what could I do? I said goodbye to the cats and got in the canoe and we went down to where the helicopter was landing. There were six men on that helicopter and then me. Have you ever been in a helicopter? Well, this one didn't have any doors on it and it took them about ten minutes just to strap me in. First time I ever been in a helicopter.

"They brought me to the airport and then I was on a plane that took me to Arkansas. We were at an army base, Fort Chafee, near Fort Smith, Arkansas. Now by this time I hadn't eaten anything except a peanut butter sandwich the day before. So we get there and they want to feed us, but I couldn't eat what they had. Honey, I wouldn't give this food to your dog. It was this macaroni, not even warm and with no gravy on it. So I said no thanks. Everywhere you went people were handing you water, so I figured I'd just fill up on water.

"Well, I find a bus and it takes me into Fort Smith, into the town. But now it's Labor Day weekend. I had completely forgot about the holiday. All the stores were closed, even the little lunch counter at the bus depot. But someone there says you can get a meal at a place a few blocks away. So I'm outside walking, hauling my bags and wondering if I'm even going to make it a few blocks because I haven't eaten in so long. And that's when this girl pulls up in her car.

"There must be an angel watching over me because every time I really needed something there was someone there to give it to me. Just like that girl with the canoe outside my house, here comes this other girl, and she gives me a ride to the restaurant. So I get in and she brings me to the restaurant. And do I eat? I had eggs and bacon and a waffle this thick with butter on top. It looked like an ice cream scoop of butter and it melted all over it. I just ate and ate. Every time the waitress came by I asked for more coffee, even if I wasn't empty yet. Before I knew it I had three cups of coffee.

"I noticed that the couple sitting behind me was looking at me. You know how you can see it out the corner of your eye? And I thought, 'Oh well, they probably think I'm a bag lady.' I have all these bags with me and I'm eating like I haven't eaten in days. Well, I figure I better turn around and say hi so they know I'm okay. They said hi back and asked if I was from around here. I said, 'No, I'm from New Orleans, Louisiana.' And the man says, 'Oh! I've been there, I know New Orleans! Which neighborhood?' I say Mid-City. And he says, 'I know there. Carrollton Avenue and Canal Street!' And I say, 'Boy, you do know it.'

"So later on the waitress gives me the check and I bring it up to the cashier and I give her the check and I give her a ten-dollar bill. And she takes the check but pushes back the money. So I push the money back to her and she pushes it back again. And I push it back again, and this time I look away, like maybe she doesn't want me to see her take it. But she pushes it back to me again. So I say, 'Well, what's going on? I'm trying to pay.' And she says, 'You can't, it's already taken care of." And you know what? I think those people I was talking to signaled her or something and took care of it.

"I'm back now. I'm living out in Metairie with my girlfriend and her boyfriend. She gave me her little Mercedes to drive since my Cutlass was flooded. She wants me to buy her car. You know what? It's a piece of junk. You can't drive it! I miss my Cutlass. That first big boat that came along to get me in the flood ran into it and broke the front window. I know it was flooded, but none of the windows broke until that boat hit it.

"I'll be back as soon as I can. You will too? That's so good to hear, babe. We need to get people back in the neighborhood. I don't care if I have to drive to Metairie to get water and do errands. I don't care about the inconvenience. I just want to get home and live here again. Does your dog want a little biscuit?"

She produced a dog biscuit from her pocket and adroitly flipped it into the Amazing Dr. Watson's mouth. I took out my camera and asked Miss Anne if I could take our picture together.

"No, baby, no," she said. "Look at me here with my hair curlers in. I'm in no shape for a picture."

But I insisted and she relented. First, though, she had to put on her sunglasses and the breathing mask she had for working in her house. It would be her disguise, she said, so no one would know how she looked with her curlers in. I reached my arm as far out as I could, pointed the camera back at us and we put our heads close together for the photo. Between her oversized breathing mask and her big, cat's-eye sunglasses, the only parts of her face to be seen in that picture are the little crow-claw creases around her eyes that let you know she has a big, broad smile underneath it all.

Three   Heartbreak Motel

I had no family stuck in the city to worry about when the storm struck. Nobody I knew drowned in an attic or died on the sidewalk waiting for diabetes medicine. I knew most of my friends had left, and even my dog was safe with me. But in the aftermath, what I worried about most was my neighborhood—a mixture of people, buildings, history, and geography that had stolen my heart, anchored me to a now-crippled place, and drew me through the muck to return after Katrina.

My life in Mid-City began in 2002 when I met Minnette Patterson—or Mrs. Minnette as she preferred to be addressed—and saw the beautiful but tattered house she wanted me to buy. I moved to New Orleans from Rhode Island in 1999 because I wanted to live in a place that felt like a foreign country but where I could still speak English. I was right on the first count, though only half right on the second, since I hadn't accounted for the hybrid accent (more Long Island than Deep South) and the rampant use of a local parlance so particular it could merit its own Crescent City Rosetta Stone. I initially rented an apartment in an Uptown neighborhood, but when I wanted to buy a house I turned to the Mid-City area where real estate prices were much lower.

Mrs. Minnette's house was a two-story double, which meant I could live in one side and rent the other to cover a good part of the mortgage. Though weathered and neglected, the one-hundred-year-old place was captivating even at first glace. To me, the house looked like one of those downtrodden girls with bad posture and low self-esteem who just bloom beautifully once they get a healthy dose of love and attention.

The floors are heart pine and the woodwork is all Louisiana cypress. Up front, the house has stained-glass windows of yellow, pink, and pale blue in half-moon patterns that look like a geisha's fan. It has columned mantelpieces in the living room and dining

28

room with mirrors embedded in each. The ceilings are ten feet high in every room to soak up some of the summer heat, and the house is raised on piers almost four feet off the ground since, of course, everyone knows New Orleans is liable to flood a bit from time to time.

Buying the house from Mrs. Minnette was an intimate experience. She was seventy-eight, and we were introduced by friends who lived next door. She would not use a real estate agent, and she would not list or advertise the place as being for sale. She just wanted to sell the house to a nice man who would fix it up with the energy she could no longer provide. Mrs. Minnette showed me the house herself while her husband waited in the car with the air conditioner running.

"Would you be a dear and help me a bit on these stairs?" she asked. I held her arm and gave her a little boost as we walked up the stairs of her house.

She hadn't lived in the house for decades. She had moved out to the suburbs and had rented the place to a succession of increasingly troublesome tenants as the neighborhood tumbled into an economic decline. Over the years, the house had been cut into four apartments through a series of inexpert renovations, which added flimsy paneled walls and patched over the large, graceful flow of doorways and corridors between rooms. An upstairs bedroom had been turned into a kitchen, though it still looked more like a bedroom with a few extra plumbing fixtures and some lame vinyl floor tiling than a proper kitchen. Mrs. Minnette stood near me on our tour and gave each room we entered a slow, heavy review, like she was inspecting a family photo album extracted from the forgotten corner of the attic. We hadn't even discussed money yet, but already she was talking about the house as if it were sold, asking me what I planned to do with a particular room and whether I'd repaint the exterior.

We wrote the sales agreement freehand on Mrs. Minnette's dining room table at her house in the suburbs while her husband brought us cans of root beer from a fridge in the garage. It was hard to believe that our handwriting on a sheet of paper would be official and somehow entitle me to own her house. But it stuck; the closing attorney we later visited blessed it with stamps and seals, and in the end she handed me a metal ring holding more than a dozen keys to the various locks and deadbolts on the house. It cost literally every penny I had, and after we signed all the final paperwork the closing attorney was good enough to give me five dollars so I could buy a hamburger for lunch. But I was in. I owned the house.

About a month after the sale, Mrs. Minnette called to check up on me.

"Did you get that apartment side rented yet, sweetheart?" she asked.

"Not yet, but two girls are coming by to look at it this weekend."

"Oh, baby. No. Not girls. Don't ever rent to single girls like that."

"No?"

"No, no. One time, I rented that side of the house you're living in to girls. Guess what? I'll tell you, Mr. Ian, they ended up being prostitutes. They were using that house of yours as a house of prostitution. I had to get the sheriff to put them out! Last time I ever rented to girls."

I am a sucker for the silent history of buildings, especially the ones where I've lived. With her bit of well-intentioned advice, Mrs. Minnette had given voice to one small, priceless piece of this one. I wanted to know what had happened in the old house's rooms during all those years and generations before, and not just the salacious stuff like prostitutes working in my present-day dining room. I wondered what sort of clothing people wore when they lived there in the 1920s, what they did for jobs in the 1930s, whether they kept hooch around somewhere during Prohibition, if they watched news reports from the Vietnam war in the living room on new color TVs. To me, the house was more than a real estate asset or a place to live. It was my own little piece of New Orleans, a tiny part of a legendary place that had a past before I came along and a future with me in it.

The house needed a great deal of renovation work, which required ripping out walls, digging plumbing out of the muddy ground underneath it, filling in termite-gnawed floor planks, and replacing brittle, antique electrical wiring. Because I had spent every penny to wedge myself into the house, I had to do much of this work myself and, since I had little building knowledge, that meant a lot of trial and much more error.

But along the way I ended up knowing the house well, and not just its structure. I felt like I was earning my place in its history through my work to restore its health and well-being. I felt that, down the line, after I had moved somewhere else and even after I was dead, other people would be living there within the same walls. It was part of my own story, and I was a part of its story too, and to me this gave it something like a soul. I had fought with this house and cursed it on hot days when I was covered in sweat and dirt and bleeding here and there where it had bitten me with nails and splinters, and I had rejoiced within it and because of it when my work came to fruition and when I could have people visit under its roof. I respected it and cared for it. I made sacrifices for it and was happy having it in my life. It was a relationship.

Things were going well in Mid-City before Hurricane Katrina. The old streetcar service was restored along Canal Street, replacing the city buses, and new businesses were opening along its route. There was a healthy boom in house renovations on the streets nearby, and real estate values were rising.

Mid-City is home to some of the oldest New Orleans restaurants outside of the French Quarter, with a collection of casual Creole joints like Mandina's and Liuzza's, an old Italian ice cream parlor called Brocato's and the best steakhouse in town, the Crescent City Steakhouse. The New Orleans Jazz & Heritage Festival (Jazz Fest) takes place at a horse track nearby, drawing a few hundred thousand people to the area each year. At Mardi Gras time, the largest parade in the city passes right down Canal Street a block from my house like a rolling, interactive circus.

But Mid-City was no idyllic village. Drug dealing was beyond blatant. Before I had lived in my new house for a month I knew where the drug dealers lived and I knew the cars of some of their most devoted customers. Petty theft and armed robbery seemed to be a weekly double feature on the police blotter for the area. The sushi deliveryman was robbed on his way to my neighbor's door. My tenant's car was stolen from the street outside our house one night. A mugger had staked out the sidewalk approach to our corner pub, Finn McCool's, and would periodically rob people on their way out.

"On the way out! Now how stupid can you be? Who ever walks out of a pub with more money than he walked in with?" I exclaimed one day while sitting at Finn McCool's bar.

"Yeah, if this guy would just rob people on their way in he'd get twice as much money. Then he'd only have to mug half as many people," said my neighbor Trent McGill, whose arms are covered in tattoos of Elvis Presley. He had been mugged outside the pub a few nights earlier. "Muggers just aren't too fucking bright," he said, shaking his head with real pity.

The criminal activity in Mid-City was infuriating, but it never succeeded in running off anyone I knew. These problems were troughs in the flow of the neighborhood's lifestyle, and the compensating peaks were much higher and lasted much longer. For instance, Finn McCool's might have been a target for a while, but that couldn't diminish its luster as a symbol of upward progress for the neighborhood. The old corner bar had been called Joe's for ages. It was ready to fall over in a pile of rotten splinters at any moment, and the only question was whether the regular coterie of afternoon drinkers there would just dust themselves off and continue sipping their beers amid the rubble or move on and find a new place to spend their retirement checks.

But in the same year I bought my house around the corner, a group of Irish immigrants took over the bar. They were from outside Belfast and had been slinging drinks at pubs there since grade school. In New Orleans they had worked all manner of jobs for years and earned enough money along the way to buy their own place. They renovated Joe's into something that looked like a real Irish pub, renamed it for a hero of Celtic myth, and essentially transformed it from a blight into a Mid-City asset. Neighbors from all walks of life caught up with each other there, and people from across the city gathered for the parties they threw. They showed European sports games on satellite TV, and the place quickly turned into the clubhouse for the city's expatriate community. On Sunday afternoons when the New Orleans Saints were playing, Katie the redhead barmaid would lead the crowd in cheers and chants during key plays

and throw herself into full-fledged cartwheels behind the bar between mixing bloody Marys and drawing off draft pints of Guinness Stout. To celebrate their Irish heritage, the owners each year
host an event dubbed "The World's Shortest St. Patrick's Day Parade,"
complete with a king and queen chosen from bar regulars, a baby
dressed as a leprechaun, someone posing as St. Patrick himself, and
a route that begins at the pool table, flows through the front door,
and heads straight back in the side door about ninety seconds later.
It was a participatory pub.

The neighborhood's beautiful old houses, reasonable real estate
prices, and colorful community life drew an endlessly interesting
mix of people. My neighbors Michael and Becker can be counted
on to show up at a Mardi Gras party in full face paint, and at Halloween, Michael greets trick-or-treaters at the door dressed like a
medieval executioner. People occasionally hire brass bands to run
their own mini jazz parades around the neighborhood to celebrate
or proclaim something or other. Mr. Frank was a long-retired sheriff's deputy who made a nightly patrol of our block with aromatic
pipe smoke marking his slow, shuffling progress, a long flashlight
in his hand, and at least one pistol on his person. Sometimes when
I came home in the evening I would find him sitting on my front
steps, taking a smoke, catching his breath, and surveying the street.
Back at his house, he had hung a life-size plywood cutout of a go-
rilla from the gable and periodically added more of his seasonal,
holiday-themed cutouts to the façade. My neighbors Errol and Peggy
are the local public television station's on-air color commentators
for Mardi Gras parades and high society balls and are prolific au-
thors and editors of New Orleans lore and history. Mr. Don was a
retired merchant seaman who kept a tiny apartment behind a big
house on the block primarily so he could stay close to the horse
track a mile down the road. He is over eighty years old, had a plastic hip courtesy of the veterans affairs hospital, and, between the
local horse racing seasons when he had more free time, he dated
prolifically among a pool of women who were born well after he
had completed his World War II maritime service. One street over,
Harold Brown, the former drummer for the 1970s funk band War,
would turn his porch into a stage for an annual summertime block

party where anyone at all was welcome to jam, from teenagers with Stratocaster knockoffs to Sunpie Barnes, a former pro football player turned local zydeco accordion star.

If there was a little backstreet parade going off, I knew I would find my neighbor Keith Hurtt there, sometimes dressed for a safari in straw hat and hiking shorts, sometimes ready for a masque ball with a parasol and a top hat. Keith is just a bit younger than my father, and I can hardly keep up with him. He has lived in New Orleans for most of his life and is so deeply marinated in the lifestyle that I'm sure he would have perished from cultural dehydration if he were forced to live anywhere else for very long. He served in the navy, but only long enough to acquire a love for seafaring songs, which he has committed to the aural equivalent of a photographic memory he has at his command. He holds countless songs in his head—the older, longer, and bawdier the better—and, like a jukebox stuck in a time warp, he can produce any of them at the slightest prodding.

Keith is a criminal defense attorney, and when business was slow he was known to pay late-night visits to the twenty-four-hour bars in our neighborhood and pass his cards around to the glowering or unsteady barflies there. "Keep this in your wallet, friend, you might just need it someday," he would tell them.

Keith came back to New Orleans as soon as he heard a few bars were open down in the French Quarter. He made his own trip through Mid-City not long after O'Brien and I had paddled through its flooded streets. By then, enough water had been pumped out that he could drive his little convertible up Canal Street, but the water was still standing a foot or so deep in the blocks around our houses.

"My wife says our ground floor was half full of water," he told me when I finally ran into him a few weeks after the storm. "But I'm an optimist. I say it was half empty."

I wanted to get back to Mid-City very badly, even though I knew its horrid poststorm condition would likely persist for a long time. Baton Rouge was dealing with its own flood of displaced New Orleans people. If things had settled into a surreal manageability back in New Orleans after a few weeks, Baton Rouge was still an evolving crisis of too many people and not enough of anything they needed.

When New Orleans evacuated, Baton Rouge was the first city most of its people came across, and many of them went no farther. We doubled the population of Louisiana's capital city literally overnight to about five hundred thousand, and there was simply no place left to pack people in.

When it became clear that no one would be returning to New Orleans anytime soon, people snapped up apartments and condos, and some even bought houses. But most of us, dazed and unbelieving, lingered wherever we had landed until the housing stock was bulging beyond capacity. Relatives piled up in homes all over town, their cars parked five and six deep on lawns. There was a run on lumber at hardware stores as people began building lofts and bunk beds in their living rooms for their stranded kin. Dorm rooms at Louisiana State University were packed with parents getting an early return on the investment in their children's education.

The small Baton Rouge convention center became a shelter for thousands. There were so many people in the downtown streets around it that the police closed the surrounding blocks to traffic. People slept in their cars. Parking lots at stores, parks, and offices were filled at night with people in clunkers that barely managed to make the drive to Baton Rouge and sputtered on the verge of engine failure with every trip to the next parking lot.

Motels filled up even before the storm hit. Companies had reserved blocks of rooms for their employees, and the families who randomly found rooms on their own were not budging. The government might pick up their tabs, the Red Cross might help out, but in any case there was nowhere else to go so the credit card meter had to keep turning.

The haven of Kathleen Lousteau's generous house in Baton Rouge spared me from the initial hotel hunt. But when it was obvious that our stay would be much longer than anyone first thought—with those first wild predictions of New Orleans remaining uninhabitable for as long as six months—I knew I had to find more permanent digs.

Hardly anyone seemed able to get answers—much less money—from insurance companies, so a lot of us just started sharing whatever resources we could muster. My friend Whitney and I threw our lot together on the housing front. She was also staying at Kathleen's house with her two small dogs. We were surprised to find that the newspaper offered some options. We could assume from the listed rents—$400 a month for two bedrooms, $250 a month for one bedroom—that these apartments would be in seedy areas, but we were stoic. We were from New Orleans, we assured ourselves, so how intimidating could suburban Baton Rouge really get?

"Stay away from presidents or Indians," counseled one of Whitney's local Baton Rouge friends. "Any street named for a president or an Indian is going to be bad."

But these were desperate times, so we didn't think twice about circling ads for apartments on streets like Choctaw, Madison, Chippewa, or Washington. They panned out very badly, and we reached our nadir checking out one place that had been advertised simply as "house, 2 bdrms, kit., ba., $175/mo." We found it down a side street named for an Indian tribe where the blocks denigrated from lousy to scary.

"Well, it looks all right around here," Whitney said hopefully as we turned off the main road. "Just kids playing ball in the street. Who cares?"

The next block got bad. Men standing in the street stared at us hard as we drove past their small, dilapidated houses. The third block was our destination, and we pulled into the driveway of our address. The house was a breadbox. There were the remnants of sheets or tattered towels partially blocking the windows. The paint was peeling on the weatherboards like a bad sunburn. Something that looked like silver spray paint had been applied roughly around the windows. The yard was a mess of knee-high weeds. The house seemed practically to buzz and tremble with all the bugs that were surely seething inside it.

"Should we take a look?" Whitney asked.

"I'm looking," I said.

"I mean look in the windows," she said.

I got out of the car. The house next door was similar, but in worse shape even than the specimen of decrepitude in front of us. There was a plastic tarp lean-to erected over part of the yard, and a group of four or five men shaded themselves from the midmorning sun beneath it, sitting on an assortment of folding chairs and milk crates. Half of them were bare-chested, and all of them were sucking on quarts of beer. They stared at us in disbelief.

I waved. One of them lifted his quart bottle in my direction as acknowledgment, and they all continued staring. Whatever conversation they might have been having was still hanging there, paused, in the air.

I looked at the house again. There were no air conditioners. I gazed at those ghostly looking sheets tacked up in the windows. I pictured nights spent slapping bugs and rubbing itchy welts. I saw our dogs pacing around nervously, barking at rats. I saw faces watching our comings and goings and imagined a break-in and losing the meager contents of our evacuation suitcases. We had to find somewhere to live, but we would have to find a way other than this. I got back into the car where Whitney was waiting.

"Fuck this place," I said, watching the guys next door under the lean-to watching us. Whitney drove us away.

Then there was a lucky break. Another displaced friend called from the Quality Suites motel where she was staying. It turned out her family owned the place, and, even though it was packed to overflowing and companies were calling around the clock looking for open rooms for this or that vital, displaced employee, she told me there was a room we could take.

"But here's the deal," she said. "It's messed up. No AC, some of the furniture is broken. They're trying to fix it, but it's taking a long time. They can't get parts, and no one will come out for a small job like this right now. But if you want it, it's yours."

I didn't have to think about it for a second. I packed up quickly and was there within an hour of the phone call. I told Whitney, and she arranged to meet me there the next day. The room was indeed trashed. It looked like a failing rock band had taken out a night of midtour frustration on it. But a room to myself, a stable home base where I could start planning next moves or just escape for a while, was a new luxury.

I don't know how, but the next day when I returned to the motel from work, we had a different room. Whitney had arrived with her little dogs, and we had been transferred to a fully functional room. It was really two rooms. The front room had a couch and chairs and a table, and the next room had two big beds separated by a nightstand, complete with a factory-fresh Bible in its drawer. It was on the third floor, and the view from the window lined up perfectly level with the highway just outside, which was a solid mass of cars and trucks for most of the day. We could look outside and see drivers losing their minds behind the wheel, stuck in the crazy post-storm congestion of Baton Rouge bursting at its seams with unhappy, homeless New Orleans people, insurance and construction people, media and government workers, and everyone else with a stake in the disaster eighty miles downriver.

By the time Whitney and I and our three dogs got there, the Quality Suites had been home to many of its guests for several weeks, and it was already starting to show. Quite a few people can sleep in a motel room when they have to, it turns out. The two double beds could sleep two each, the sofa pulled out to be a bed and could sleep two more, and then there was the remaining floor space for air mattresses and sleeping bags, bringing the grand total of people sleeping in some of these rooms to perhaps eight extended family members. But sleeping is one thing, and being awake and cooped up with that many people is something else, living with all their open suitcases and damp towels and bathroom habits and crinkling bags of nervous munchy food and crumbs.

No one would like this situation, but many New Orleanians entered it with a unique adaptive advantage from our natural habitat back home. One of the most common house designs in New Orleans is the shotgun. These old and historic houses can be beautiful, but the arrangement of their rooms is an anachronism compared to compartmentalized modern designs with master bathrooms and open kitchens. In a traditional shotgun, one room leads to the next in a long, straight line. They are said to be as straight as a shotgun barrel, hence the name. To get from one room to another in a shotgun house usually means walking through other bedrooms or living rooms. So if Junior sleeps in the front room and he wakes up in the middle night and needs to take a whiz, getting to the bathroom could mean barging through rooms of territorial siblings or parents who may at that hour be in the throes of a strangely affectionate wresting match.

Families who live in shotgun houses come to regard privacy as a luxury only available through radical renovation. But virtually all shotgun houses have front porches or stoops, and these become the outdoor living rooms and common ground for their residents. On many New Orleans blocks, sitting outside on your porch means seeing neighbors next door or across the way sitting outside on theirs.

The New Orleans people stranded at the Quality Suites quickly replicated this neighborhood environment in the spaces they found at the motel. The courtyard became the communal park, like a college quad. People dragged the padded, institutional motel chairs from their rooms outside and clustered them around their doors where they could take the air and talk and smoke all night long.

Walking by with the Amazing Dr. Watson, his claws skittering on the motel pavement like those of an alien species, I would see entire family dramas play out there as if on sidewalk display. There was the mother fidgeting with cigarettes and the father slumped low with a beer can between his legs and his face impassive as his brain worked over insurance policy math equations. The door might be open to their room, revealing a mess of strewn clothing, towels hung on doorknobs, pizza boxes, and shoes everywhere. There would be the teenage daughter on the sofa, pouting and upset and silent. The younger boys would be running around outside, chasing each other with bright plastic baseball bats. And then there would be the puppy with a sock in his mouth, tied by a leash to the mother's chair and ducking the ash falling from her twitching cigarette.

People installed barbecue grills all over the motel property, and sunset brought group cookouts in the courtyard and on walkways of the upper floors. People took to washing clothes by hand in their motel room tubs and hanging them to dry outside on little runs of string tied to the landscaping and walkway railings. Walking to my room, I would pass their wet shirts and jeans and undies strung up there in all sizes from little sister to fat uncle.

Dogs romped around in the courtyard too, usually leashed but sometimes breaking formation to beg at a grill or inspect another dog. Motel management had driven a stake into the grass in the center of the courtyard and hung there a stash of plastic bags for guests to use in cleaning up after their dogs, an extraordinary accommodation from a business that had a brass sign reading "No Pets Allowed" posted at its front desk.

On hot nights, the view from the third-floor walkway outside my room was like a look into the heart of some subtropical commune with extended families intermingling in the courtyard, meaty smoke rising from a collection of grills, dogs chasing each other and children chasing the dogs, and parents lolling beers, crying on each other's shoulders out of despair and stress and wiping their eyes to holler at the dogs and children running about.

Every person I knew from New Orleans was also displaced and staying with family or friends or in motels or apartments secured by their employers. We joked darkly that the worst part of the whole experience was that even after all that had happened to us, we could not complain about it because someone else we knew was in a far worse situation.

"We lost our homes, we lost our neighborhoods, some of us lost our jobs," the joke went, "and if that wasn't enough, we lost our God-given right as Americans to complain about it."

I knew my house had been flooded, but other people's houses still were flooded and some were completely gone. Some people could not find relatives and friends, and others were pretty sure some people they loved were dead. I was staying in a motel with my dog, while others stayed on cots on the floors of basketball arenas and on sofas in church libraries and in their cars at rest stop parking lots.

Even if I began to feel sorry for myself after a long day working the phones and sitting in traffic and contemplating life in indefinite exile, a quick walk past the other rooms at the motel cured the self-pity. I would pass the families on their makeshift stoops again, with the doors open to the crowded world of their motel rooms with the laundry and air mattresses and antsy kids. At lights-out time, I imagined such rooms as an orchestra of family snores and wheezing.

The season of evacuation crept into its fifth week, and October emerged on the calendar. Displaced children living in the motel began attending schools in Baton Rouge. Some people started taping their kids' school papers to the motel room windows that were facing out to the walkway. Other guests and the motel housekeepers passing by could see their crayon drawings and assignments graded with little stars and smiley faces drawn in the corner by the teacher's pen.

The longer I stayed in Baton Rouge the heavier the question of home and its fate weighed on me. It was a source of gut-wrenching anxiety, something so big and so important to my identity and to my vision for my life in the future that no line of thought could avoid running into it. Most of my friends felt something like the same way. We were all waiting for answers, for some word about if and when and how we could go back to our all but quarantined city, but there was nothing coming. What official guidance we could find seemed more theoretical and political than anything that could answer the question of home that loomed over us. It was like a suspended anvil, something that had to drop eventually, and the only question was if it would fall just behind our heels as a near miss or if it would land on our heads as a crushing blow.

The only thing that helped was actually going back home on those weekend trips, seeing the old house and being on the familiar streets, however distorted they were now. What little work I could do on my early visits with the bleach mop and the claw hammer was as much catharsis for my sense of displacement and helplessness as it was therapy for the damaged house. I felt real pain each time I left, driving back to Baton Rouge at the sunset curfew, inching west in the intense daily exodus of flatbeds and work vans and emergency vehicles, watching the city recede in my mirror as the radio talk shows featured one tear-choked caller after the next.

I decided I wouldn't wait for any official green light to signal my return home. I knew it was possible to repair my house and that most of my neighbors could repair theirs too. I couldn't wait for insurance money or backlogged contractors when I knew I could sleep in my old bed on the second floor of my own house in the heart of my own city. I learned that my office would reopen downtown by the end of October as the company's first symbolic return to its city, and that one practical consideration sealed the deal for me.

I had no illusions that simply returning would restore some kind of normalcy, some sense of that longed-for life that existed before Katrina made landfall. Even someone blind to all the wreckage and deaf to the sounds of demolition tractors and the sobs of disconsolate neighbors inspecting their homes still could never miss the smell and even the taste of the place, that low-level, omnipresent murk. It painted a foul, salty background over everything, like a glaze of residue and rot punctuated occasionally by the outright exclamations of organic reek from toppled refrigerators and unremediated grocery stores. But still, the road to normal had to start somewhere, and it surely never would if I stayed in Baton Rouge watching the seasons change with the themes of the displaced kids' school drawings taped to the sad windows of their parents' motel rooms.

There was also an argument for civic duty. Someone, after all, had to be the first one back in each deserted neighborhood, on each empty block. I didn't know my neighbors' plans, but I knew that with no kids to worry over, with my job intact and now local again and with a relatively unscathed second floor of my house to live in, I could come back before a lot of others. When my neighbors came to visit their houses, I wanted them to see that the recovery was already starting to happen, that people were back, or at least a person was back. With no official plan forthcoming for Mid-City, it would be up to individuals to return and weigh the benefits of reinvesting their lives or walking away. So instead of my neighbors coming home to utter desolation and deciding to cash out in sorrow, I polished a positive fantasy that they would arrive to find me walking my dog along our street, fixing my house, offering them a cold one from the cooler.

Then there was the specter of looters. With so few people in the city, there were still some who were ransacking even flooded homes for whatever they might find on upper floors. There was really very little of any value left in my place, but the thought of looters breaking into my house or my neighbors' houses, the thought of that continued violation, was just too repugnant. So by returning early I could also add to my proud little list of recovery roles the title of "sentinel," a watchman for the wreckage.

More than anything, though, I was compelled by my own personal desire to make it real, to live the experience of my city in a way that watching it on TV, writing about it in countless e-mail correspondences, or even seeing it firsthand on my weekend visits never could. I needed to immerse myself in home and be part of it, even in its pain and degradation.

I wasn't interested in living anywhere else. It would feel like a betrayal. It would feel like turning my back on someone I loved because she had been attacked and raped, like walking out on her at her most desperate and vulnerable moment. That's when you need to love the most, I told myself, that's when you need to affirm the value of life and the wonder of beautiful things. New Orleans was my beautiful thing.

I wrote out all these rationales one night in Baton Rouge, sitting in a huge, high-backed booth at a chain restaurant in a strip mall. It was getting toward closing time when I arrived at the restaurant, but the hostess sat me anyway in the back of the mostly empty dining room. I was all but cloistered by the padded heights of the booth, and I must have succumbed to the quasi-private setting because immediately the barometer of my heart fell to emotional lows. I ordered dinner from the young, pretty, somewhat worried-looking waitress, and then brought out a notebook. I started writing down the reasons to return home, essentially making the case to myself to live again in the city I loved, and I soon began to cry.

The waitress arrived with my glass of wine and found me deep in teary introspection, gazing across the table at the empty side of the booth with my face flushed and wet. I tried to get myself together. I drank half of the wine in a gulp and went to the restroom to wash my face. I returned to the table and my notebook and tried to focus on something practical. I made a list of supplies I would need to buy before returning home—candles, lantern oil, water, a spare can opener, more bleach, batteries, first aid stuff— and promptly resumed crying.

The waitress seemed increasingly wary each time she returned to bring a salad or more wine. She approached the table with the cautious, grossed-out delicacy of a first-year zookeeper assigned to feed one of the more dangerous animals. I might even have been snorting at one point or another, probably around the time I came up with the analogy of New Orleans as a raped lover I mustn't abandon. Eventually the waitress came around with the bill, hovering just beyond the line she might have assumed was the reach of my claws or tentacles. I looked past her and noticed that parts of the restaurant were already being cleaned up for the night in a clatter of forks and water glasses and a rumble of stacked barstools.

"Do you want anything else?" she asked.

I really must have looked like a wreck, puffy-eyed from crying and hunched over my little notebook with my abysmal dinner sitting cold and only half eaten off to the side. The waitress looked down at me wide-eyed. I wondered how many other New Orleans people were stuck at that moment in rooms around Baton Rouge or in Atlanta or in Houston, stranded with no prospect of home, crying in front of people who might sympathize but who would never get it at all.

And then, in an instant, I had a whole new reason for getting back home in a hurry. No matter how bad it was back in New Orleans, I told myself, I would at least blend in with all the other basket cases.

Four Omens of Homecoming

My friend Peter Reichard worked up this little saying a few years back, during the public relations run-up to the war in Iraq. When a calamity somewhere in the country made the news, he would point out its potential meaning as an omen of bad tidings. I think he got it from a flip comment someone made to him in passing, but it struck such a chord that it attached itself to the collective parlance of our group of friends. We would hear of some terrible event and the refrain would be "In another culture, you know, they would call this an omen."

The world was certainly providing Peter with plenty of material. As the government readied itself to go to war overseas, the space shuttle Columbia exploded on reentry, raining bits of aerospace technology and astronauts down over a vast debris field in the president's home state of Texas. In the same season a deadly stampede occurred at a Chicago nightclub, and it was around then that pyrotechnics at a heavy metal concert set a Rhode Island music club on fire and killed more than a hundred people.

"In some cultures, you know, they would call this an omen," Peter would say. I had his words in mind when I made my return to New Orleans after my two-month exile in Baton Rouge.

My company was moving a tiny bit of the workforce back to its big headquarters building in downtown New Orleans, and my position was among them. Some of my coworkers would commute from whatever housing they had found outside the city. My house was still wrecked, as was Mid-City, and it didn't matter a damn to me because I was heading home.

But on my last day in Baton Rouge, my happy excitement was somewhat clouded by an argument I was conducting with myself. I sat at work for a good portion of the day staring at the computer

45

monitor, while in my head I was turning over the pros and cons of just running down the street to buy a gun.

I had never owned one. Of the handful of instances when I'd pulled a real trigger, I was either wearing a Boy Scout uniform at camp or was deep in a field of someone's farm, shooting at cans with a responsible, card-carrying adult overseeing it all.

The advice of my old friend Rene came to mind throughout the day. Rene, it should be said, was an ex-con who seemed always on the verge of becoming a current con. At the time, I was just about to buy my house, and Rene and I were discussing issues of owning and protecting property. I had never been in a situation where having a gun would have helped me in the least. I had been robbed at gunpoint once on the street near my old Uptown apartment, but having a gun at home would have done me no good. Even if I had had a gun on me—as if I would pocket the thing for a simple walk around the neighborhood—I couldn't seriously imagine myself pulling it out and escalating a mugging to a shootout over the contents of my normally depleted wallet. I was open to the reasonable arguments against gun ownership—that a gun in the house is far more likely to cause an accidental shooting than anything else, that it could fall into the hands of a criminal during a robbery and raise untold mayhem.

But Rene was not concerned with such reasoning. To him, the question was being prepared. If I was buying a house, it was going to have a door, and to Rene's thinking I had better be prepared to face whatever might come bursting through that door. In Rene's life bad things had a way of bursting through doors far more often than most people would expect.

"All your nice friends'll think you're a psycho for having a gun in the house," he told me. "But if you need one and you don't have one you'll be feeling pretty fucking stupid."

He hadn't convinced me at the time to buy a gun. But the rationale I held against the idea came from the assumption that civilization was holding a net in front of my face that could catch a cannonball. Returning to flood-ruined New Orleans in late October, I was working under the assumption that the net had a lot of unseen holes in it to begin with and was altogether gone now anyway.

Truly, the months after the evacuation were the longest the city had gone in modern times without violent crime. With only a sliver of its former population back, there was a Pax NOLA in effect during that fall. But I had been in my neighborhood by myself on those earlier weekend visits. I had seen people crawling around the debris piles during the day, and wondered where they got off to at night. I had looked down blacked-out streets and wondered what I wasn't seeing, I had lain awake in my upstairs bedroom and wondered what I wasn't hearing outside. Anyone who happened to pass through Mid-City knew there was no electricity and no alarms. There were no phones except cell phones and these had only the most iffy service and limited battery power. I would be living in a wood and plaster shell with a friendly dog and nothing but goodwill and fear keeping anyone at all from coming in through a broken window. It seemed like the right situation for a gun.

At the end of that final day in Baton Rouge, I left the company's temporary headquarters for the last time, drove half a mile through gridlocked traffic, past the ordinary fast food joints and ordinary car dealerships and ordinary furniture stores, and parked in front of an ordinary building packed with guns and ammo.

I had tried to bone up a bit on gun terminology by reading some gun reviews on the Internet. I came across a few chat rooms with illuminating postings about what a burglar would look like if hit at close range by birdshot. Someone had posted a message giving his wife's physical measurements and asking for opinions about the size gun she might enjoy most as a Christmas gift. He got plenty of detailed responses, most pointing the way toward 20-gauge shotguns. The consensus among this particular group of online correspondents was that a 20-gauge shotgun would allow the wife to blast someone in the same room without peppering anyone on the other side of the wall with stray pellets.

I walked into the Baton Rouge gun store thinking that maybe a 20-gauge shotgun was the one for me. This was all very new to me. I wasn't even sure just what that sort of gun would look like.

"Well, what do you want it for?" asked the man at the counter. He was tall and trim with a buzz cut and an intense, squared-off bearing that said ex-military. He had a tattoo on his wrist like an Iron Cross, the German wartime military decoration. He was eyeing me with what I thought was suspicious concern, like I was asking for a club membership I hadn't earned.

"Home defense," I said, repeating a term I had seen referenced endlessly just that afternoon in the online chat rooms.

"Well, the 20-gauge is a woman's gun," he said. "You're a big guy, you can handle a 12-gauge."

A 20-gauge sounded bigger than a 12-gauge to me, but I thought it better to keep that to myself. The clerk grabbed a black shotgun off the rack behind him and laid it on the counter between us. I picked it up and examined it with feigned scrutiny. I had no idea what I might be looking for to differentiate this gun from any other in quality or potential customer satisfaction.

"Of course," the clerk said, "if you want home defense, you might as well just buy a .45. That's what I got. That'll do it for sure."

"But I want the . . ." I was searching for another term I'd just learned online. "The, ah, intimidation factor. You know, that pump action sound to scare someone off." I imitated the sound of a pump action shotgun for him out of the corner of my mouth. "Cha-chunk."

I was at the moment holding an actual, unloaded pump action shotgun, but I hadn't yet figured out how to pump it even for the purposes of demonstration. I half-tried, but when it was clear the distinctive sound wouldn't just emerge from the gun with my fiddling I stopped in midmotion. The clerk seemed to recognize what I was trying to do and looked at me with real scorn.

"Yeah, well, it's your money, but if some asshole is ballsy enough to come into your house you better just shoot him and not mess around with sound effects."

I made my selection. It seemed obvious I should take the shotgun he had already pulled down from the rack. I filled out a registration form that asked about half as many questions as the typical patient survey at the dentist's office, and he took my ID into the back room. I waited around examining all the other guns in the cases and the stuffed game mounted on the walls. He returned a moment later with my ID and our completed paperwork.

"All set. You need some shells?"

In a minute I was handing him my credit card at the cash register. And then I was out of the store, walking toward the car with a 12-gauge shotgun and a stash of forty shells.

Back at the Quality Suites, I burst into the room to find Dr. Watson sprawled as usual on the bed.

"Come on, boy, we're getting out of here," I bellowed at him. I was so excited, I felt like I had to tell someone.

My bags were already packed, so it was a quick transfer to the car. Now the trunk was filled with my newly acquired weaponry and all the canned food, candles, ice, beer, and dog food I could fit in it. I checked out of the motel, ceremoniously handing the key back to the clerk and officially turning over my room to whoever would come along next.

"I hope you come back and visit us again," the clerk said.

I couldn't believe it, but I said I did too and I really meant it. I really could envision a return visit, under different circumstances, when the visit would be simply for nostalgia, a trippy one-night get-away from a busy, revived New Orleans. I hoped I would be back with a woman and that we would stay in the same room 314 where I had droned away too many angry nights staring at the blank ceiling and fretting over a blank future life without New Orleans. It would be a victory lap.

On the highway, the car peeled away the miles, and I was practically counting them down in my excitement. We turned a great bend in the road right around the parish line at the border of the city, and the downtown skyline appeared in dark silhouette, the skyscrapers standing tall but blacked-out in the grim distance.

Soon, there appeared a riot of flashing emergency lights just ahead by the side of the road. As we drove closer, the lights composed themselves into fire trucks parked at random angles on two lanes of the highway. Just past them was a huge blaze. I thought it was a burning car at first, but the fire was far too big. I slowed down and in a moment came to a full stop on the highway in front of a house engulfed in flames. The house was beautiful, the kind of structure known in New Orleans as a center hall Creole, and true to form it had a wide sweeping staircase leading up to a deep, covered front porch supported by columns. It must have been built around the turn of the century, long before engineers cut through its neighborhood and made it highway frontage property.

All of it was awash in fire. The entire structure was red and orange and black with the flames and smoke, as if it had been some blank white form colored in by the messy strokes of a toddler with a handful of autumn tone crayons. The fire was intense. I could feel the skin on my face tightening as the heat beamed in across the highway and through my open car window. There were perhaps a half dozen fire trucks parked around it, plus a few police cars, but no one seemed to be doing anything about the blaze. Clearly, the house was doomed by this point. I saw the shapes of men standing around the fire trucks, watching the flames consume the old, beautiful wooden structure. The hot highway was illuminated by the flashing lights on their vehicles, but otherwise everything around the burning house was in darkness.

It was like a torch left at the city gates, a burning bouquet staked out here as a twisted welcome home greeting to my mangled and broken city. It dropped a cold bucket of foreboding into my stomach.

"In another culture, you know"—I could hear Peter's refrain in my head—"they would call this an omen."

I pulled off the highway about half a mile later, took the usual turns and was in front of my house. The block looked just as it did at night on my previous weekend visits, and there was the same swampy smell and moist feel of the air. Still, I took a long look around this time, now that I was returning for good. As before, there was no sign of anyone, not even the hint of a light anywhere. I pulled into the neighbor's empty driveway to get the big car off the littered road and let Dr. Watson out. He hopped down from the backseat but stayed close by me as I hauled our gear back into the house. I lit a bunch of candles, piled the canned food on a work table in the living room, brought in the shotgun in its cardboard package, and our beachhead was complete.

I spread out an old sleeping bag for Dr. Watson to lounge on, and he settled into it rather quickly, tucking his legs underneath him and surveying the familiar old room. I left the front doors open after bringing in my bags. There seemed little point in shutting them, and

I wanted anyone who might pass by to know I was home. I brought a hurricane lamp outside and left it lit on the edge of the porch just in front of the door. It was only after I set up this little flickering proclamation of return that it occurred to me that I should at least familiarize myself with the shotgun, now about three hours in my possession. I delicately opened up its packaging and read the instruction booklet by candlelight.

My battery-powered radio was tuned to WWOZ, the little non-profit station that is practically the daily soundtrack of New Orleans. The station was still having broadcasting problems from whatever remote site its producers had found after the flood, so sometimes between songs there would be a long silence. These awkward breaks were only intensified by the lack of other competing noise. A song would end and for half a minute or more there would be nothing. Just when I began to wonder if the broadcast would resume, another song would snap on or the DJ would do some talking. The DJs at WWOZ were not professional radio business personalities broadcasting from afar. Rather, they were volunteers and local people who were neck deep in the same awful situation we were all dealing with, people who had wrecked homes and lost futures. Their voices cracked with emotion when they spoke to their crushed community over the airwaves, offering little messages of encouragement to keep on believing in their city.

I was growing a little more comfortable with the workings of the shotgun. I finally figured out how to load it and then set it aside on the table, beside an oil lantern lighting up my dining room. An old R&B number wrapped up on WWOZ, followed by the DJ's uneven voice reading the list of songs he had just played. Then he said: "It's ten p.m. and this is WWOZ signing off. Tune in again at seven. Goodnight, New Orleans." The radio went silent, and it was a half hour before I realized nothing else would be coming on again.

Halloween came around three days after I returned home, near the two-month anniversary of the storm. After eight weeks of incomprehension and despair and rage, after two months of life as refugees or evacuees or victims, the people who came creeping back into New Orleans bumped up against what is normally one of the city's favorite holidays. No one was ready for a holiday, but here it was and we had to deal with it.

If there's one thing New Orleans people love more than holidays, it is dressing up in costumes for holidays. Only Mardi Gras trumps Halloween in the quality and quantity of costumes. Kids go out trick-or-treating and adults host house parties and there are costume balls, but most of all people congregate in the streets of the French Quarter and the adjacent neighborhood, the Faubourg Marigny. They stroll around, they duck into bars, they hang on the corner—and always they show off their finery and check out others' creations.

The first post-Katrina Halloween had virtually no reported incidents of sincere trick-or-treating, primarily because there were scarcely any children in the city whatsoever. There were no schools open, and most the people who were back were not bringing kids in tow. Trick-or-treating for any of the few kids within the city limits would have yielded slim pickings anyway. Most houses remained empty even in the neighborhoods that did not flood, as people sorted out their job options and decisions to return or begin building a life elsewhere. So trick-or-treating was out, but it was clear that the adult parties and the French Quarter street scene were definitely on.

Halloween coincided with my first day back in my downtown office. There were something like two or three dozen people in that first wave of workers returning to a twenty-two-story building designed to accommodate hundreds. Leaving the house that morning for work, I felt as though I was getting an early start on Halloween. I was back in my normal prestorm routine, riding my bicycle downtown and working in my staid office for the day, going out for lunch and biking back home again. But now every part of that routine was distorted by Katrina, as if I was going through my old daily pattern draped in a grotesque costume. I took a shower that morning and it was ice cold. I walked downstairs to a kitchen without gas or electricity for anything. I biked down Canal Street, and it was so empty of traffic I could ride right down the middle of the road instead of being pinned against its shoulder by hurtling buses and commuters running late, as normally I would be.

The workday was hardly about work. It was more like the first day back in school for seventh graders inspecting their new desks and lockers. We were all back in our offices and at our desks for the first time in two months, staring at yellow sticky notes and project lists and appointments inked onto our wall calendars from August, before our world stood still, tilted on its axis, and dumped all its contents into the cauldron. The desktop clutter was not exactly nostalgic, but I did stare at a checklist of tasks I had planned to get done on the day Katrina hit as if it was some kind of museum exhibit of carefree days. Outside, a huge trailer-sized generator was supplying power for the old building, and in the washroom none of the plumbing fixtures quite worked right. The office itself was quiet as we all sorted through our old work places, and above us most of the other twenty-one floors sat empty. Throughout downtown, most of the big office buildings were also deserted, and when we went outside the streets and sidewalks were as empty as a soundstage set cleared by the director for a lonely scene.

When the day was over, I straddled my bike again and headed back home. Darkness had almost completely fallen for the night. I pushed the pedals up the two miles of Canal Street to my neighborhood, and along the way I was passed by perhaps five or six vehicles— all trucks, and all of them contractors with extension ladders jutting out the backs of their tailgates and drywall dust flying out in comet trails behind them.

Back home, it was costume time for real. If you live in New Orleans for a year or more you will almost certainly accumulate a costume box. This can be any sort of container—usually at least the size of a steamer trunk—and it holds all the flotsam and jetsam of previous costumes, all the wigs and capes and bits of fabric and masks and hats and feathers. With a reasonably well-stocked costume box, you can dress for any sort of costume affair on short notice and even accommodate ill-equipped visiting guests. My costume boxes came through the storm and flood safely in my attic, and, riffling through them by flashlight, I pieced together a workable pirate theme with a puffy shirt, black tights, a thick leather belt, a long, straggly red wig with a black bandana, and a Jolly Roger flag I fashioned into a cape. I posed for the dog, who looked up indulgently from his sleeping bag. I was now properly attired for a party being held, incredibly, just one block away by my neighbors Justin and Kiersta, two doctors who dish out pro bono medical help almost as often as they throw costume parties.

Their old New Orleans house had been flooded after the levee failure, and they were now living in an apartment in the Irish Channel. But they are virtually addicted to costume parties, so they decided to shake things up a bit by hosting one in their flood-wracked house. They were in the midst of gutting the ground floor of their beautiful two-story Victorian. Most of the walls were ripped out, exposing the skeletal framing to offer views from room to room and clear across the floor plan. Candles and lanterns were the only illumination, and guests walked up from the dark street awkwardly, dressed in costumes and wearing doubtful expressions. The party was a general warm-up for whatever else people had planned later on that night. Still, there was a bowl of candy at the door. On my way inside, a woman dressed as a cancan dancer told me the candy was set out as a hopeful gesture for trick-or-treaters.

"They're not expecting any, of course. You know, who's living around here? No kids, right?" she said, laughing.

"Maybe it's good luck even still," I said.

"Maybe you're right!" she said cheerfully. "Maybe it's like a talisman, like leaving a sacrifice. Candy in effigy! No one eat it! No one's allowed to eat this candy!"

And no one ate any. Everyone seemed more interested in walking around the ersatz haunted house. It looked creepy, no doubt about it. Gutting is a violent term, and it is an apt one for the process of rapidly emptying a house of everything in it down to the framing studs. It looked like something terrible had happened here, like the insides of this once beautiful place had been sucked out by some unstoppable force. The flickering candlelight helped make the scene even more disconcerting and ominous.

Amid this, the good humor and hopeful attitudes of the group shone through. Justin was dressed as an MRE, the military combat rations, or "Meal Ready to Eat," which on his costume stood for "Male Ready to Eat." A box of brown paper encased his torso, and all the familiar markings and labels from the real MREs we had been eating were drawn on it very studiously in black marker and modified for the bawdy theme of his costume.

His wife, Kiersta, was decked out in the uniform of a Girl Scout in training, a Brownie, and the joke of it was that she was a "Heckuva Job Brownie," a mocking echo of President Bush's assessment of FEMA director Mike Brown's performance as the agony of New Orleans was in full crisis.

A good costume needs a punch line, and mine was that I was no ordinary pirate but a corporate pirate, swashbuckling away with fatted government contracts for disaster recovery. Later, downtown, there would be whole packs of people dressed up as discarded refrigerators, usually made from the boxes of the new refrigerators they had just bought to replace their pestilent old ones. Blue tarps, now so common on our shredded roofs, were ubiquitous on the costume trail as well. One woman had fashioned an impressively feminine getup from the rugged blue plastic, forming it into a bustier complete with lace-up trussing woven through the tarp's metal grommets, nylon rope shoulder straps, and a plunging neckline revealing the majority of her barely contained breasts.

Two months after the storm, we were able to make jokes through our costumes, but the ire was always close to the surface. I knew the laughter Justin and Kiersta shared with us at their party was only a thin mask for their anxiety. We were celebrating the holiday in a house emptied of everything, decorated now only with their friends in costume and candlelit smiles. They had no idea if they would be able to work again as doctors in their city, or if their neighborhood— our neighborhood—would ever resume the life it had so vividly lived before the storm.

The party wrapped up as people began to filter out and head downtown for the rest of the night. I brought Dr. Watson home, pointlessly instructed him to attack or at least bark at anyone who might prowl by, and set off on my bicycle in my pirate costume toward the French Quarter.

I could have taken my car, and for once parking in the Quarter was certainly not going to be a problem with so few people back. But riding a bike had long been part of my daily New Orleans lifestyle and was something I couldn't do during my exile to the suburban sprawl of highways and feeder roads that cut up Baton Rouge. Pedaling around my city was something I had missed and one of those little things I insisted on doing again as a declaration of return.

I was not yet accustomed to the utter and overwhelming darkness of my neighborhood at night. It changed everything, including
my assumptions about where I should and should not go. Before the
storm, I had developed a few normal biking routes I considered safer
than others. They were primarily along the main streets that offered
shoulders for a little buffer against the cars and good lighting or at
least the security of other people in transit. None of that counted
now, and even on my weekend visits I had begun to experiment
with new routes between my house in Mid-City and the promise of
lights and people that beckoned downtown. I took side streets past
block after block of shotguns and cottages, many of them rundown
for years but most of them attractive with the weathered resilience
of well-designed, historic buildings. Before the storm, some of these
routes would have been too hostile and menaced by thugs to safely
bike through, but now there was something exciting in the freedom
to go down any street I pleased, even if it was under circumstances
of darkness and abandonment.

I was about six or eight blocks into my Halloween trip, rolling
down Bienville Street past the dark façades of one- and two-story
houses. The continuous horizontal stain of flood lines appeared in
bold strokes. They were high up, showing the terrible depth of the
flood. It seemed that no one had even been back to begin clearing
out these houses. There were no telltale piles of debris outside their
doors, just destroyed cars and tree limbs that still lay where they
had fallen in the storm.

Up ahead I saw the light of a small fire burning in a barbecue
grill in front of a flooded-out Laundromat. I could see three or four
people in silhouette standing around the fire. They were the first
sign of life I had seen since leaving the party, and I greeted them
with a clang from the bell attached to my bike handlebars, its happy
little grating tune the only sound in the night.

"Who the fuck is that!?" A man's voice rang out roughly from the
group of dark shapes. I rang the clanging bell again.

"Just a friend in the night," I called out over my shoulder.

"All right then," a voice muttered back, but it wasn't friendly. I
pedaled on and crossed a major street without slowing. There was
no traffic coming or going. A grocery store was on the opposite

corner, and I could smell the reek of spoiled food coming from its rotting bowels before I had even crossed the street.

The next few blocks were lined with nice, big oak trees that stretched their limbs toward each other from either side of the street to form a dense canopy overhead. The street was now pitch black, and I had to slow the bike and strain my eyes to spot potholes or sharp debris just in front of my rolling tire.

Then I heard the dogs. There was a single, sharp bark—like an alarm—followed by the response of two more barks from different animals in quick succession. I looked over to see three low, dark shapes shoot out from the shadows around a blacked-out school building. They were running toward me at a lightning clip across the schoolyard, moving with the lunging speed of beasts in pursuit. The next sound was of a speedy scamper of their many legs and claws hitting the pavement on the street behind me. My innards went cold and my head flashed hot as I realized in an instant what was happening. Stray dogs, gone half feral by now, I imagined, scavenging and hunting in the putrid wasteland they'd been abandoned to, and they were coming after me. My feet exploded on the pedals, my ass in the air pushing them as fast as I could and my hold on the handlebars death-grip tight. My big old beach cruiser bike had never felt so heavy, and as I pedaled desperately I wished I had some light speedster instead of this fat, flashy thing. Better yet, I wished I was in my car. I could hear the animals behind me growling as they ran. I read somewhere that dogs are silent just before they attack and that a growling or barking dog is still making up its mind whether to run away or rip your arm off. But with the bastards at my rear fender that bit of zoological trivia did not come to mind.

One of my top personal fears has long been getting arrested while wearing a costume, of being processed off to jail for some reason dressed in tights or covered in face paint, and now I seemed on the brink of being mauled by angry, starving dogs in the dark while dressed as a pirate. My cape was straight out behind me and my feet, wrapped in white rubber fishing boots, were circling as fast as possible. I didn't dare look back now for fear of breaking stride. I could see nothing immediately in front of me—just the moonlight falling a few blocks ahead where the dark canopy of oak limbs let up. I flashed through an intersection without a thought of oncoming traffic and kept at it. The dogs fell back, spent, and I heard one or two of them give me a few salutary barks as I pedaled away.

My bike continued to whiz over the street that had miraculously not thrown any ruinous obstacles in my path for the two blocks of blind fury I had pedaled through, and my speed slackened as my feet stopped pushing. I was breathing hard and shaking. Up just ahead was the elevated highway, and on the other side were the downtown neighborhoods that meant civilization and people and lights. I felt like I had just sprinted no-man's-land back to a friendly trench. The hellhounds had slunk back to their pathetic dens in the shadows. Farther back, those silhouette figures by the Laundromat were no doubt still standing around their barbecue fire cursing at anyone else who might pass by. Back home, two miles deep in the darkness, I knew my dog was lying on a sleeping bag in my empty rooms, my new shotgun was sitting loaded by my canned food and lanterns, and somewhere the DJs on WWOZ were getting ready to play their last song for the night.

Peter's voice was in my head again. "In some cultures, you know, they would call this an omen," he was saying about it all.

Five   Candles & Coolers

I've always felt that the great, weathered old buildings of New Orleans are part of the city's landscape in the way that mountains and bays define other towns. Their old bricks and lumber seem groaningly alive. Their many details in woodwork and stained glass and plaster, though the craft of people, nevertheless come across a hundred years or so later as beautiful manifestations of nature, like crystal formations or the intricacy of a mottled iris. But I also think the buildings need people living inside them to animate their old bones and bring them to life.

The Amazing Dr. Watson and I were back home for good now, but the chill of that long spell of inactivity in the house after the flood still hung in each room of the place. Even under normal circumstances, if I took a trip for a week or so it always seemed like there was some minor but detectable difference when I first walked back in and dropped my suitcase, like maybe everything had somehow settled without anyone moving around inside the house for a while. Now there was something much stronger and odious. I had swabbed the place with bleach, scrubbed everything down and cleared out all the rotting fabrics and food, but this didn't have anything to do with odor or mold spores. It was something psychic, something from the heavy, tangible, and certain emptiness that had laid siege to the house for two months.

Maybe it was creeping in from the streets, from the vast pool of emptiness that surrounded my little homestead. Certainly, the house was more porous and vulnerable to intrusion than ever, with its missing windows, pocked roof, and loosened doors, and there was plenty enough abandonment outside to press its way in. I knew it would take something special to throw it all off. Getting rid of this malaise was the rallying cry for what I billed on the invitations as the Candles & Coolers Party.

* * *

Prior to the storm, I had people over on the slightest pretext, be it a Mardi Gras parade party, a crawfish boil for someone's birthday, or even a group viewing of a televised political campaign debate. A video store rental, an extension cord leading to a TV on the porch, and a healthy dose of DEET were enough to declare an outdoor movie night party. The Candles & Coolers Party would be my first social gathering without the benefit of electricity, but I actually found myself enjoying the preparations. Certainly, I felt a sense of purpose. I wanted to import people to the neighborhood. Many of my friends were back in the city, but all of them lived in areas that had not flooded very badly or at all. They had great difficulties, but they also had neighbors and lights. A few months after the storm, it seemed possible to drive around and pretend everything was all right in New Orleans if you just stayed Uptown. When I visited Uptown at that point the intact neighborhoods seemed worlds away from the disaster area of my blocks and my life.

Mid-City remained just as dark as it had on my earlier weekend visits, still covered at night in that inky, engulfing dark that turned our voices to involuntary whispers when we were in the thick of it. There were dead, flooded vehicles everywhere and skeletal magnolia trees and piles of jagged debris and streets spiked with upturned roofing nails practically aiming for car tires. This was where I had invited people to come for a party, but I thought perhaps the setting would be just weird enough to draw my hardcore New Orleans friends through it.

Most of my flooded furniture from the first floor now sat in a broken heap on the sidewalk out front. This left the downstairs rooms stark, but I regarded that as a blank canvas for party decorations. The dining room is situated in the middle of the house, and as soon as I had moved back it became my de facto command center, the place where I stockpiled my food and lanterns and arranged whatever pile of insurance paperwork I happened to be wading through. The legs of the dining room table were flaked apart by their long flood soak, but the tabletop was okay, so I amputated the legs and replaced them with a pair of sawhorses as prosthetics.

I stacked my varied and colorful collection of canned goods on this table, as well as the plastic bowls and utensils and matches. I was just trying to keep everything close together so it would be easier to see in dim light, but in the process I had built a stylized altar of groceries—black beans and tuna fish and spicy stewed tomatoes and field peas—all illuminated delicately by the glow of decorative candlesticks and oil lanterns. It was like a Campbell's Soup and Tupperware version of the edible St. Joseph's Day altars some Italian families around New Orleans make each year.

I was pulling out all the stops for illumination at the party, making my own wax and wick lightshow around the rooms. I crammed tapers and votive candles everywhere possible. A pair of iron candlesticks shaped like elks' heads flanked the canned food gallery, while tea lights flickered at varying levels across the tops of stacked cans, like a pretty city skyline in extreme model miniature. Since the sawhorse table was the brightest spot in the house, I arranged the coolers nearby in a little campus pattern. Out of necessity I concentrated the food, beer, and light together and in the process inadvertently discovered a solution for house party hosts everywhere who lament that all their guests inevitably wind up crammed in the kitchen. The answer, made so clear by post-Katrina accommodations, is simply to cut all power to the kitchen, rip out all cabinets and countertops, wheel the fridge to the curb, and stock nothing in the room more appetizing than bleach bottles, tattered mops, and dog food. If anyone ventured back to the kitchen during the party, it was merely to inspect the damage and quickly return to the dining room or porch. I had actually decorated the kitchen with a pair of lovely little candles burning on the ruined stovetop, but it didn't seem to inspire anyone to linger back there.

The house was fully aglow after my party preparations, and I had some leftover candles, so I decided to take a few outside to try to light the way a bit. I set burning candles on the filthy, flood-streaked washer and dryer I had rolled out from the shed to the curb earlier that day, and they made such an instant improvement to the outdoor scene that I ran back inside and collected more candles to distribute. After still another trip back in for more candles, I found myself poaching some of my earlier indoor displays. But it was worth it, because the effect outside was really coming together. I put two Catholic prayer candles on the roof of the flooded Honda Accord sitting grimly just outside my door. I put a lantern on the sidewalk down the street and set others on assorted household debris piles here and there. I even put a few on the steps leading to some of the neighbors' kicked-in front doors, as if they were home and participating in this ad hoc neighborhood lighting ceremony. Soon, the block was thoroughly dotted with little glowing beacons.

At every party I have ever thrown, in New Orleans or anywhere else, there is always a moment when I wonder if anyone will actually show up. The drinks would be iced, the house decorated, some carefully chosen music would be playing on the stereo, I would be dressed up and ready to welcome friends. And while I was standing there, cutting into the first drink, the thought would invariably arise that perhaps no one would come after all, not out of malice but simply from some fluke of social calendars and whatnot. The Candles & Coolers Party, of course, intensified the awkward premonition that I might just spend the night alone here with the dog, too much beer, and too many candles. A simple drive around the city's debris-strewn streets presented a startlingly high chance of picking up a flat tire, and there was a fairly well-established mania about the health risks of even visiting houses that had flooded. Mold was said to be pulsing invisibly everywhere, and according to some people it was as toxic as mustard gas. Plus, the curfew in my zip code had only just been revised from 8 p.m. to 2 a.m., and news of such official adjustments had a slow and distorted way of traveling around town. Maybe everyone would just stay Uptown.

But people did show. The sound of a solitary car carried easily along the empty streets, and I was so attuned to the hoped-for sounds of approach that when the first one rounded the block I might have heard it even before Dr. Watson. As it was, the dog gave no sign of excitement as one after another familiar car took the turn onto my block—this was not, after all, the arrival of the mailman—but I was practically pressing my nose against the front window craning for a look. A few people had already shown up when I spotted my friend Keith Hurtt and his wife, Dee, walking down the street. Keith was carrying an oil lantern in front of them and in its glow they looked like country farmers from another century strolling across the dark acres to call on their neighbors. They came inside and joined everyone else inspecting the damage and ongoing repairs to the house like peculiarly jovial insurance adjustors. All of us had newly acquired skills at eyeballing room dimensions, ballparking replacement costs, and accounting for policy claim restrictions, and we engaged this new hobby every time we entered a flooded New Orleans house. There was certainly no trouble getting conversations started at this party, even before the booze kicked in.

The gathering had grown to a proper party when I noticed a van picking its way down my street, defying the now pointless one-way traffic sign. The van slowed in front of my crowded porch, and young, smiling faces beamed out its windows. I thought they might have been friends of friends dropping in on the party, but then one of the people inside called out to us.

"Do you need food?" she shouted cheerfully. "We have plenty!"

They turned out to be relief volunteers, cruising the neighborhood with Styrofoam crates of warm meals cooked at an Uptown church kitchen. It occurred to me briefly that maybe accepting donated dinners for my house party—and delivered to the doorstep, no less—might be a little greedy or indulgent when I already had a candlelit stockpile of canned beans and tomatoes. But then again, these people were not going to find many other takers for their food around here. Keith and Dee were the only people I knew about staying in the whole area, and they were already at my party. Maybe the volunteers had even been drawn the wrong way down my street because they saw the candles in the darkness and wanted to get rid of their load of food so they could get on with their night. Besides, the food was probably getting cold.

"Sure," I yelled back, "we'd love some food. And why don't you come on in for a beer?"

"Thanks! But we're underage!" one of them called back.

They loaded us up with eight or ten cartons of food, which we opened to find ravioli in a thin tomato sauce with slices of white bread. From a nutritional standpoint, it was the salvation of the party. I had made practically no attempt to provide any kind of meal for the event. I encouraged people to take anything from the collection of canned food they wanted. Someone opened a can of tuna fish and someone else tried the black beans with a heavy dose of Tabasco, but otherwise the response to the canned buffet was lackluster. So the church ravioli delivery from the underage volunteers proved to be a welcome addition.

Wherever two or more from New Orleans were gathered in the months after Katrina, talk of the storm was certain to be there. We had house repair talk, and we could grouse over the insurance companies. There were also questions about where you rode out the storm, the status of your job, and all the other sundry topics that consumed our collective attention without lapse. That was the case at the Candles & Coolers Party too, though I suppose the setting didn't do much to distract guests from the crisis at hand. Still, we all agreed that the house actually looked beautiful by candlelight, which gave everyone that complimentary luster while also obscuring all the damage. So we stood around, with the front doors wide open and the windows still covered in the painted plywood storm shutters, and we talked about which neighborhoods had taken it hard, when we thought people would be coming back, and which companies were likely to abandon the city. We also talked about the silver linings for which we yearned in the aftermath. The city's perennial, interlocked problems of a corrupt public school system, a street crime culture, and devious but always reelected politicians had seemed so insurmountable before the storm, but now, we hoped, perhaps they were all susceptible to serious reform as the city rebuilt everything from the ground up.

My friends Gordon and Stacy Russell brought their five-year-old daughter, Quinn, to the party. I'm not sure I have ever seen Quinn without some sort of costume. She always seemed to have on some kind of superhero outfit or cape, even if she was merely joining her mother for a few midday errands. Tonight was no different, and she came with her parents to the party dressed in a panda bear outfit. The presence of a child within the city limits still qualified as a compelling conversation piece in November, and Quinn made a splash. She stood on top of a beer cooler to get a better look around the room, chewing a pistolette of French bread someone had brought, and, regal in her panda suit, entertained the visits of various adults who wanted to talk to her eye to eye.

Just outside, great mounds of debris were piled up like ramparts on either side of the street. In front of my house were my ruined appliances, a tangle of rusted bicycles, tentacles of tubing and pipes, the dented and dirty hot water heaters, small bushes ripped from the once landscaped ground, and disintegrating sheets of torn drywall. The swath of darkness around the house was miles deep in all directions. Inside, though, we were stoking the old gaiety and fellowship with laughter and hugs and encouragement by the light of fifty candles and several hundred cans of beer.

As is normally the case at a good house party, the Candles & Coolers Party boiled down to just a few of us clinging to the rest of the night. The evening had an unnatural limit with the 2 a.m. curfew then in force, and most guests left much earlier. By midnight or so, it was just my friends Peter and Kimberlee and myself. I had already renewed some of the candles, but most of the tea lights had burned out.

We went outside to look around at the night. Only a handful of the outdoor candles planted on the debris up and down the block remained lit, and they looked ghostly, pulsing a bit near the end of their wicks like will-o'-the-wisp in the darkness. The night sky had unveiled its uncanny crop of starlight, and the little radio inside the house was only barely audible from the street. I was feeling grand when I began to sing along to "St. Louis Blues":

I hate to see that evening sun go down
I hate to see that evening sun go down
'cause it makes me feel like
I'm on my last go-round

I put my leg up on the bumper of one of the destroyed Hondas in front of the house, and with just a step or two I was up on its hood, crunching around on the flood residue coating its surface. I gingerly inched my way up the windshield to the top of the car, straddling its sunroof. It felt like a stage and the idea caught on quickly. Peter hopped up on the other sedan just across the street. For the next hour or so, the three of us rotated around the two car tops and the sidewalk, trading solos and sing-alongs for any tune that came into our heads. We hoisted candles and sang into them as though they were microphones. We slid playfully down the slopes of dirty wind-shields as if the wrecked cars were ramps and platforms on the set of a Broadway musical.

The Amazing Dr. Watson lay on the porch, impassively watching our antics without lifting his head from the floor. There were no neighbors to complain about the noise or the dents we were mak-ing in the ruined car roofs. There was no one else around at all be-sides the occasional patrol of National Guardsmen, the headlights on their grumbling Humvees visible for blocks away like lanterns in a mineshaft.

The party ended on a soft note. One Humvee patrol came along, passed by without even stopping, and we shortly brought the cur-tain down on our car-top act. Peter and Kimberlee went their sepa-rate ways, and I blew out all the remaining candles and crept into bed upstairs happy that the party was a success. I had filled my house with people and crowded out the emptiness. I decided I would do it again in a few weeks.

The lapse of time between the parties had taken its toll on every-one and on the city. After a month back home, nothing seemed to have improved at all or even changed much except that now people were moving from shock at their surroundings to a quiet depres-sion. If there was any fascination with the novelty of living in disas-ter land, of seeing the previously mundane put through unbelievable contortions, it had settled into grim, sickening everyday fare as the weeks passed without progress or answers or direction.

Each day when I rode my bicycle downtown to work, I pedaled past a plastic dog crate abandoned on Canal Street. Through the metal bars of its little gate I could see a dog corpse splayed inside, decomposing very slowly in a lump of black fur and putrid liquid. Someone had scrawled "dead dog" on the side of the crate in black marker. I had no idea what to do about it, who to call or who might care or be in a position to take care of it, so I did nothing and the thing became a fixture of my morning commute for months. It was a graphically open totem on the street, but really just one of the countless silent horrors that lingered and lurked in neighborhoods where every building and every life in them had been violently dis-rupted and left to rot. In a way, the whole flood-gored area of the city felt like a giant car wreck that we were compelled to look at once but then forced to review day after day without remedy.

I could slowly feel myself turning a bit psychotic after a month of stress and worry and blacked-out domestic life. There were nights when I would stare at my face in the bathroom mirror by candle-light and recite a little mantra of self-encouragement. I told myself aloud that I would not lose it, that I could handle it and that I had to handle it, and that things would get better. I told myself that if I was aware of turning psychotic then I surely was not.

I knew I was drifting from a lot of my friends, and in fact I was consciously pushing away some of the people I had held close before the storm. I wished them well, but at the same time I felt I couldn't afford to keep things up on the social front. I had a budget of mental and emotional energy, and I had adopted a wartime economy of the psyche to ration them. Like kids hording scrap metal and women foregoing stockings for the sake of paratroopers, I was keeping whatever mental resources I could muster for my own personal home front campaign.

Somehow, though, I still wanted to host another party. It was adverse to my whole emotional rationing scheme and would be like a big splurge I couldn't mentally afford. But I still really wanted to have people back over. The neighborhood was just as bad off as it had been a month before. There was no one else living on my street. The first cold nights of approaching winter had made annunciations, and there was no sign of electricity or streetlights or gas for hot water. And no one—not the newspaper, not the energy utility, not city hall—could offer any sort of advice as to when they might become available. I was feeling abandoned and wanted to stage a reminder that some people were still here in my neighborhood. So I started spreading invitations to the Candles & Coolers Party II, a party with a serious chip on its shoulder.

This second party was much, much larger than the first. People who had come to the inaugural event brought others to the second installment. Word of the party moved through the shattered Mid-City community quickly, like dogs spreading the call of their bark from one yard to the next, and on the night of the event a pack showed up.

I was standing on the porch when I saw Charlie Blanque coming around the corner. He would become a close friend and neighborhood ally, but that night Charlie was for all practical purposes a stranger. He was a blue-collar New Orleans native with a very successful heating and air conditioning business and a whole crew of guys working under him. I had seen him around the neighborhood before the storm, but he was always on the fly. About the extent of my contact with him was exchanging quick hand waves from passing cars. But we certainly noticed each other after the storm, being among the few people then back, and when I invited him to my second party he seemed eager to come. When I spotted him from the porch, he was walking as fast as a guy trying to catch a plane and towing behind him, like luggage, a hand truck laden with a cooler full of beer, soda, and, most valuably, ice.

I was in heavy circulation early in the party and didn't do much besides exchange greetings with Charlie before I was off pouring someone a cup of cheap sangria. But a few hours into the night I noticed his voice floating above the others with its distinctive and classic New Orleans accent, an intonation described affectionately by locals as "yatty." He was talking to a visitor from New York, another stranger to me that a friend had brought to the party to experience New Orleans resilience in action.

"Well, let me tell you about this neighborhood," Charlie was saying, and I drifted over to listen too. "This neighborhood changed a lot when the blacks moved in."

My heart sank a bit. I had heard this diatribe from all sorts of people, united by nothing if not the assumption that because they are white and I am white we would naturally have common ground on race prejudices. The typical story went like this: Mid-City was prosperous, those horrid blacks took over, the neighborhood dissolves. Case closed. I'd heard it from people who had grown up in the neighborhood in the 1950s and 1960s and 1970s, and now I thought I was about to hear it from Charlie. But he was on quite a different tack.

"And let me tell you," he continued. "It changed for the better. This whole city did. You see, the whole thing with integration was that it chased off all those people we don't want to live around anyway. They all took off and moved to the suburbs. They got their own worlds out there, it's so different, you know? You got Metairie, and that's where you got your Metairians. Across the canal is Chalmette where you got the Chalmetians. Then there's Violet. Those are the Violations. And up on the Northshore, up across the lake where all those gated communities are, those are just rednecks."

Charlie by now had a small audience for his social geography lesson, including myself. He was rolling.

"See, in Mid-City we got everyone now. Or we did before this storm. I guess we will again, but who knows. We had gay guys. We had black guys living with white women. We had straight people. We had everything, and that's good because it was diverse. That's why we live here. We like it diverse."

I could have kissed him. Through the storm, the polyglot and complex story of our city's social relations had been presented to the world in terms that almost always ran toward the simplistic, distorted, and divisive. Charlie was holding forth on the subject before out-of-towners and had turned the usual racist bit on its head. Plus, he brought a whole cooler of beer and ice. I could see we were going to become friends.

Curfew was still officially in effect in my neighborhood, but at this point it was widely ignored by both the sprinkling of returned residents and the authorities on their occasional forays through the area. So the party went on later, and there was no sign of the National Guard that had been patrolling during the first soiree. As before, the remaining guests headed outside once the candles began to burn down, but this time there were about twenty of us instead of three.

My friend Justin Devilher, a talented chef, had brought a guitar and was playing it on the porch. The instrument was acoustic, but the music he was playing came right from the heavy metal songbook—angry, fast, and hard. Others outside soon joined him in percussion, availing themselves of the great diversity of debris within easy reach to make noise. Wooden spoons banged on soup bowls, metal rods raked against glass bottles, fallen oak branches thumped on the porch railings. Everyone was drunk. Everyone was also angry. It was a low-level anger that came from living in the storm-tossed town and dealing with stress after stress of everyday life and longer-term prospects. What started as beating a rhythm along with the guitar turned to pounding, tribal-like and very loud in the night outside the candlelit house. A barbecue grill someone deposited in front of the porch was now being used as a fire pit of sticks and lumber pieces, and it cast quite a bit of heat and light. There were also a few candles burning on the porch steps and a dazzlingly bright camping lantern, and altogether they threw a strange, sharply piercing light into the street as the beat of the violent music continued.

This was about the time when I think I made the fatal move. I had included what I thought was a funny little line on the party invitation, promising guests "canned beer, canned food, canned jokes." But some people read it as a request to bring beer or food, so there was a little pile of cans at the door where guests had dropped off their pantry donations. I walked outside, out to the tribal drumming on debris and heavy metal guitar and open flames. I saw a can of sliced mushrooms, a contribution from a guest I hadn't even officially met. I picked it up and threw it as hard as I could at the flank of the flooded Honda parked just in front of my house.

I hated this car. It was dead and abandoned, flooded and stinking and filthy and depressing and stuck right in front of my house. At the inaugural Candles & Cooler Party, it had been one of our stages. Now I had zapped it with a can of sliced mushrooms. I would like to report that what happened next went down quickly, too fast for me to intervene. But it happened gradually, and I was simply too apathetic to stop it.

A small contingent of gutter punks had made it to the party, some guys in their early twenties with black-painted fingernails and dressed in what looked like intentionally ragged clothing. I guessed that they were friends of friends. They had been drinking beers and hanging around this strange party with glum and long-drawn faces. But when the can of mushrooms hit the car, they reacted like it was a prizefight bell signaling round one. Someone picked up the can from the sidewalk and threw it at the car again, making a little dent this time in its crusty side panel. Then another one took the length of water pipe he had been using as a drumstick and punched it through a side window. And with the shatter of glass, all bets were off.

People were all over the car in short order, and not just the gutter punks. They were all beating on it, busting in the headlights and windows, jumping up and down on its hood and roof. The windshield gave out with a wet sound and sagged into the car like canvas. Justin kept up the heavy metal soundtrack with his frantic guitar on the porch and a few others were still banging their makeshift drums to the light of the fire burning in the barbecue. Inexplicably, one of the kids grabbed the garden hose in front of the porch and began spraying water around for a while, which somehow added another dimension to the chaos. Things nosedived further for the Honda when someone found a metal fencepost—about the size of a lance and very heavy—and rammed it under the hood. Using this as a lever, two of the gutter punks pried the hood apart. Another one concentrated on the doors, bending them back until they cracked and hung on their broken hinges limply. A rain gutter was put through the sunroof. They started on a second car across the street.

Everyone was laughing, because it was ridiculous. We were in an abandoned neighborhood, and we felt like kids stranded on an island with a broken conch shell. If there were any rules there was no one to enforce them anyway. I sat on the porch and watched it all going on. Even the mild mannered among my friends got in on the act. A friend who analyzes government policy for a living gave the windshield a few good bashes. A woman journalist in a designer blouse imparted the exaggerated ceremony of a baseball pitcher's windup before hurling a chunk of jackhammered concrete at the hood.

"Let's stick a rag in the tank and light it!" one of the gutter punks yelled.

The prospect of a fireball in front of my house finally roused me to action. I put an end to the demolition in the kind of way you might break up a halfhearted dogfight. I yelled and waved my arms and put myself between the gutter punks and the targeted car. There was no confrontation. Everyone tossed their implements on the ground and got back to drinking. Someone wandered off down the street, heading home. On the way to his car he delivered a final salute to the night by shoving a long metal pole through the windshield of yet another flooded sedan a few doors down.

The next morning I was stung with remorse. I woke up to a hangover, a house full of spilled candle wax, and the remains of murdered cars right outside my front door. The cars had officially died in the flood, but I still felt like we had been desecrating their bodies, and I couldn't stand to look at them. I felt like I had witnessed an assault and had done nothing to stop it. By the light of day, it looked like the scene of a car bombing. Contractors were beginning to arrive for the day, and I could see them curiously inspecting the wrecks as they slowly bounced down the rutted and trash-strewn street. At the bottom of the porch steps I saw the can of sliced mushrooms lying on the ground, its edges dented now from multiple impacts. I threw it in a pile of moldy drywall on the sidewalk and let Dr. Watson lead me around the corner on our morning walk.

Six   Civilization, Distilled and Deglazed

Back in September, during that first foray I made with O'Brien into the city, the proprietor of Molly's at the Market pub in the French Quarter kept the big arched doors of his old establishment wide open to admit as much light and breeze as possible. We were sitting inside the sweltering, blacked-out bar listening to the Saints game on the radio in the corner, drinking some of the beers we had delivered from Baton Rouge to help resupply the place, when a woman on her bicycle glided right in through those open doors from Decatur Street.

The fat front tire of her beach cruiser came to a gentle rest against the flank of the bar, bouncing back a pace on impact. Everyone looked up when she rolled in. With the bright, noontime sun behind her, she was just a dark shape moving into the room on two wheels. Details materialized as she drew closer. She had curly red hair and was wearing a bikini top and denim shorts—just a pretty New Orleans girl riding her bike through the Quarter on a hot day, albeit at the edge of a sprawling urban disaster under military lockdown.

She ordered a Coke from Monaghan, the pub keeper. He looked on the brink of physical collapse after staying up for days on end but nonetheless perked up for the new customer. I noticed a tattoo on the girl's shoulder. I could tell it was fresh, in part because the skin around the ink was still inflamed, but also because the design was of a red, blade-shaped hurricane symbol with a big letter K in its center. It was the first Katrina-inspired art I had seen of any type, and I asked her how she had managed to get a tattoo in the city when no one had electricity and the few remaining residents spent a good portion of their day ducking National Guard patrols.

"There's a guy in a hotel down the street, he's a tattoo guy," she said. "He's got the gun hooked up to a car battery and he's bartering. He really wants to get a digital camera or a laptop. You know, to document all this shit. If you got one he'll trade you, like, a full back tattoo or a year's worth of work or whatever. Just yell from the street and he'll throw you the key to get up there."

O'Brien had gone outside and I wandered out to tell him about the tattoo discovery. It seemed newsworthy. By the time I walked back inside Molly's, the redhead was on the other side of the bar. Monaghan was handing her a massive set of keys and showing her where all the mixers were stashed. He had hired her on the spot, and there she was, just a few minutes after she pedaled in for a Coke, running the whole bar. Monaghan went off somewhere to sleep. I asked the girl for a beer and she charged me three dollars for one of the Coronas we had shuttled in that morning ourselves.

"Exact change is great if you got it," she told me.

It was the first glimmer I had that New Orleans could make it back to something like its old self, and the barroom setting for this revelation proved significant. In the months that followed, through all the darkness and fear, the best moments of encouragement and happiness came more often from bars and restaurants than anywhere else. The city's eating and drinking places were the fires around which we circled for reminders of the city's life and culture before the storm, for company and sometimes literally for warmth.

A little corner joint called the Banks Street Bar was the first business I found reopened in Mid-City, though the conditions under which it conducted commerce were as weird and harrowing as the neighborhood around it. The place had been a dreadful dive for ages, but, not long before Katrina, a new owner had taken over and she made a lot of good changes. She started hiring local bands to play on weekends, and people from other neighborhoods began making it a destination for nights out. There was a big chafing dish of red beans and rice set out for free for the patrons on Monday nights, and sometimes on other nights there was free jambalaya. It was well on its way to becoming a really enjoyable place when Katrina hit and the levee failure filled the building with about eight feet of floodwater.

I thought I was seeing things the night I found the Banks Street Bar open again. It was early November, and around that time it seemed like there was not a single light in my shattered neighborhood except the ones I lit with matches each night at my own house. But I was walking the Amazing Dr. Watson one evening just after sunset when I noticed a dim flicker in the distance. I kept walking toward it, but even after a few blocks it didn't seem to get any closer; it was like some mirage hovering in the darkness that receded with each step I took toward it. In fact, the light turned out to be half a mile down the road, but, like the random noises in the nighttime vacuum of the streets, the smallest source of light could stand out with startling clarity from quite far away.

The dog and I walked closer, and eventually the flickers ahead resolved themselves into a cluster of candles set in a big picture window frame at the Banks Street Bar. The glass was smashed out of the window, and the sounds of a radio playing and people muttering and even the clatter of ice being pushed around in a cooler came right out to the street where Dr. Watson and I stood trying to size things up.

We walked in the door, which was swinging open on its hinges. It sounded like a generator was running on the second floor of the old building, but in the barroom itself the only illumination came from candles and the moonlight shining through the empty window frame. Dr. Watson was alert and anxious. His canine intuition must have picked up the vibe in the room, because everyone else inside seemed alert and anxious as well. If they had tails, they would have been as erect as Dr. Watson's. There was only a handful of people in the room, and all of them were sitting on stools pulled up around the pool table, their faces half obscured in shadow even just a few feet from the candle flames. Everyone was playing it cool, but they were still jumpy, glancing up quickly at our arrival and then nodding back in their half-shadows again, reaching slowly for cigarettes set in makeshift beer can ashtrays as their eyes scanned the room. The whole scene seemed just a few boot spurs and Stetsons away from a spaghetti Western saloon tensed up for the bad guy to arrive.

The actual bar was somewhere beyond the circle of light, back against the wall, while the pool table had become the de facto bar. The table was ruined by the flood and already warped at an abstract angle, but it was pushed right under the window and got more moonlight than any other spot in the room. A big woman in a sweaty tank top was running the show from one side of the table. All over the ruined green felt before her was a collection of liquor bottles and mixers, while at her feet was a fort of coolers and cardboard beer cases. People ordered drinks like they were calling out complex pool hall bank shots.

"Gimme a gin and tonic," said one patron from the darkness at the other end of the pool table.

"What kinda gin you want?" asked the bartender.

"Oh, ah, what's that over by the corner pocket, left side? That Beefeater? Beefeater's fine. And use that Schweppes tonic by the right corner pocket. That's what I like, not that Sav-A-Center crap. I know you fished that crap outta the flood!"

When I asked for a beer, the woman nodded and felt around in a cooler. She found a Miller Lite and charged me three dollars. When I ordered another beer a few minutes later, she produced a can of Guinness Stout and likewise charged me three dollars. There was no ordering by brand, I quickly learned, you just asked for a beer and the bartender went bobbing for whatever she found in the dark ice chests down below the pool table.

The flood had really hit the place hard, and it was bad inside. I couldn't see the walls out beyond the perimeter of candlelight, but I still knew they were moldy. The smell was unmistakable. I could feel it in my nose and taste it in my mouth as sharp as licking the back of an old stamp. But it didn't matter. The Banks Street Bar was open, and it seemed like a miracle. Instantly, the bar had resumed its traditional role as a neighborhood gathering place. Walking around the streets, it was hard to believe that anyone else was even breathing in Mid-City, but my dog and I had stumbled upon a room right in the heart of the neighborhood where a bona fide, if bizarre, social scene had emerged. Occasionally, a new face would appear from the darkness of the street. It was always a man, and he would look as incredulous as I'm sure I had peering in the door for the first time. But then the guy would step inside—cautiously, like a swimmer dipping his toe in the water—and ask for a drink and then settle in for a few.

Within just a few weeks, the Banks Street Bar was cleaned up, the mold stink disappeared, and, while there was still no electricity, the collection of candles and lanterns multiplied as a concentrically expanding circle of light under its roof. Eventually, some of the walls became visible from the pool table and the place grew downright welcoming, even if making a trip to the bathroom still required taking your own candle into the dark extremities of the building.

Incredibly, the bar began hosting bands again around this time. One early performer was Ingrid Lucia, a beautiful jazz singer who lives in Mid-City just a few blocks away from the bar. It was a for-real booking in a surreal place, and management even had the gumption to dub the weekly gig the "Acoustic by Candlelight Night." Ingrid sang while her guitarist played behind her, and she made a specialty of old Billie Holiday songs, including a few suddenly poignant numbers like "Romance in the Dark." She sang:

The music was so entrancing
The lights all began to fade
I said to myself keep dancing
But only my heart obeyed
A flame grew from just a spark
When I found romance in the dark with you

Candles burned all around the ruined room, stuck in spent liquor bottles and in little decorative votives with mismatched holiday themes and even on elaborate, antique-looking candelabras. People danced by the pool table bar, where the grab-bag selection of drinks still flowed for three dollars a throw. Sometimes, dancing couples slipped into the darkness at the back of the room while Ingrid kept singing by the gathered glow around her guitarist and the tip jar.

Anywhere a bar reopened in the city, people found it and gladly plunked down their cash, which was the only tender generally accepted except for the odd barter here or there. It didn't matter if the place had lights. I began to think it wouldn't really even matter if the place had a roof unless, of course, it started raining. An enterprising boy with an ironing board for a counter and the contents of his dad's flooded liquor cabinet for inventory could have made a junior fortune on any corner in the city where people might still pass. New Orleans is a town, after all, where in normal times people routinely follow street parades and jazz funerals with stolen shopping carts packed with loose ice and cans of beer, selling them for a buck or two to the revelers or the mourners as the case may be. Even before Katrina, people here were primed for unconventional entrepreneurism.

Getting the city's cuisine and restaurant scene back in working order again proved a much more difficult proposition than opening the bars, however. For a long time after the flood, a hot meal in New Orleans was generally one that came from the plastic pouch of a prepackaged combat ration, the military's MRE. They were distributed by National Guard units and at Red Cross relief stations and tossed from vans by various agencies to people on the street in a sad and grotesque reversal of New Orleans people tossing cheery Mardi Gras beads to out-of-towners on the same streets during Carnival.

If the old saying is true that there are no atheists in foxholes, then I can't imagine there are many gourmets in them either. But there were plenty of gourmets trickling back to New Orleans in the months after the storm, and despite the reduced condition of their city they turned a critical eye to the military rations. You need only visit New Orleans once to discover that food is the constant and endlessly controversial subject of conversation. Even people who have clocked out from political debate as something beyond the power of their voice or their vote will expound with great passion, nuance, and historical precedent on their favorite restaurants, from humble po-boy joints to silver-gilded Creole dining palaces. Wherever New Orleans people come together to eat, be it in a French Quarter dining room, at a picnic table in a boiled-seafood house, or even in different cities or countries on their travels, it's practically certain that food talk will spring up at some point in the interlude. For vehemence and heat, only the most intense of those call-in talk radio sports shows would come close, and even then only after the home team gave up a crucial game.

The circumstances of Hurricane Katrina could not stop this local mania, even if it did redefine for a while the terms of the conversation. Very quickly, in fact, the MRE joined the New Orleans discourse on food. The government's menu of MRE options offers different meals, identified by number, and the smattering of locals who dined on them formed definitive opinions on their own preferred and most reviled examples in no time flat. They eagerly shared their views on which ones responded best to doses of hot sauce or Creole seasoning in the same way obsessive home chefs might submit recipe feedback to cooking magazines. They soon came up with their own modifications and recipes, and these too made the rounds among the reluctant connoisseurs. Some were ingenious. For instance, the pouches and heating elements included in each MRE could easily be put to use to make a poached egg—not an easy trick to otherwise pull off in a house with a destroyed kitchen and no gas or electricity. But with an MRE and a few eggs brought in by, say, a cousin up in Baton Rouge with access to a functioning grocery store, it was simply a matter of cracking the eggs into a plastic baggie, putting the baggie into the MRE pouch, adding the heating element between the baggie and the pouch, and letting the chemical reaction do its stuff. This little science experiment produced a nicely poached egg that paired especially well with MRE menu no. 14— pasta with vegetables in Alfredo sauce. Breakfast at Brennan's this was not, but the end result was better than what was on hand at the beginning, which is, after all, the essential goal of all cooking.

"You know what this means, right?" said the woman who introduced me to this poached egg field recipe. "It means if the world comes to an end and everyone's reduced to eating these MRE things, New Orleans people will still be showing everyone else how to eat."

There was a fascination with the MRE at first, a novelty to the experience of brewing up a piping hot portion of chicken à la something in a pouch propped against a broken cinderblock on the porch. But like a lot of those Katrina experiences, the appeal wore off fast. So when the first restaurants began reopening in New Orleans, they were greeted with praise, tears, and applause.

By November, restaurant reopenings were hitting a stride in the unflooded Uptown neighborhoods and the French Quarter. Mid-City remained desolate, like the other hard-hit areas, but then Ralph's on the Park, the neighborhood's most ambitious restaurant, reopened all on its own. It was a new restaurant in an old building, and before Katrina it had already earned a reputation for refined French

Creole cuisine served in elegant dining rooms overlooking the live oaks of City Park. Ralph Brennan, the owner and namesake, is a scion of the most accomplished restaurant family in New Orleans, which can count Commander's Palace on one side of the bloodline and more than half a dozen other upscale restaurants inside the city limits alone. I was overjoyed when I heard it would reopen. Besides a handful of bars that had joined the Banks Street Bar, there were no other businesses open in the neighborhood at all. It had been much easier to find a beer, for instance, than a gallon of gas, and now with a restaurant like Ralph's open it would also be easier to find a plate of shrimp remoulade than a sheet of drywall.

I decided to celebrate on Ralph's reopening night. I dressed up in a white jacket and a fedora hat. I poured myself a plastic cup of red wine and set out for the mile-long walk through the waste-land of debris-choked blocks to the restaurant. Along the way, walking next to Bayou St. John, a huge pickup truck grumbled up beside me. It had the name of a church and a Texas address stenciled on its door. The passenger side window came down and an earnest-looking young man leaned out.

"Brother?" he said. "Do you need a hot meal?"

"Ah, thanks but I have a reservation over there," I answered, pointing in the direction of Ralph's. So the church folks waved cheerfully and drove off to find someone else to help out while I walked on to have a decadent meal of shrimp and steak and bread pudding and wine and bourbon.

Those were the dining options three months after Katrina in Mid-City, where an expensive, dressy restaurant opened long before a gas station or convenience store, much less a supermarket, would manage to come back. And it was really little wonder. Mid-City did not look like a promising business environment at the time.

That truck full of church people found me walking down the center of the street in my Sunday best because the sidewalks were mounded with stinking, jagged storm debris that stood higher than the fedora on my head. The neighborhood could only look worse if it was either still flooded or actively on fire. Most big corporate companies and chains headquartered out of town were not taking risks on the area just yet. The only businesses making early reinvestments were the small ones owned by locals. And even among them, the first few back had to gamble that their work would somehow be rewarded by someone in the crippled city.

It was. Through November, a succession of restaurants opened in Faubourg St. John, a section of Mid-City built on a higher ridge of land where the flooding had mostly added up to just a skim of water. Each time one more restaurant reopened there, the scene in its dining room was like a social roll call for the neighbors who were back.

That was the scene at the reopening of Lola's, a tiny Spanish restaurant on Esplanade Avenue. Lola's has an open kitchen, a BYOB policy, and a chef from Barcelona named Angel Miranda who lives in a house right next door. It is immensely popular with its neighbors and, before the storm, a wait for a table was almost certain unless you arrived right when the doors opened for the evening. I rode my bicycle to Lola's the night it reopened and got there just in time to join the ad hoc BYOB cocktail party that materialized on the sidewalk outside. Every table was already jammed, and a dozen people were milling around outside, drinking wine and beer. It was like a family reunion, and of course everyone kept the single, shared conservation going, which went something like "what happened to you, where did you go, what are you going to do now?"

By this point, people could pull off the hard-boiled attitude and talk tough with each other. We could talk about flooded houses and vanished jobs and what it was like to live on a perverted uncle's sofa for two months and about whatever runaround we had endured from those bastards with the insurance company or the government, and the whole time we could keep it together. Once we were at our tables inside, though, we melted.

Lola's does not serve New Orleans food, as most people know it. There's no gumbo on the menu, no red beans or etouffee or fried oysters. But it was New Orleans food to us because we knew the menu at Lola's by heart and it was our neighborhood restaurant. It was a place that, for at least a little while during the darkest days of the city's flooded, burning calamity, we thought we would never see again. That was back in the terrible time when we also thought we would never see our neighborhood again, at least not in any functional way, and that meant never seeing our homes and our city and its restaurants and our friends and neighbors.

So when the bread and aioli arrived, when the paella and garlic shrimp and snapper ceviche were set down on the table, our tears showed up too. It wasn't a big, demonstrative group sob, but all over the room people quietly wiped back tears with their napkins and loudly toasted each other around the table in voices rattled and shaken by emotion. There were pledges to never leave, or to come back soon, or to keep on fighting the forces we could feel lining up to take turns on us now that we were brought low, the politicians and insurance men and clucking pundits.

At one point, the room sharpened with the sound of just one spoon tapping a water glass for attention. As if at a wedding, people dropped their conversations and looked around to see who might be calling for a toast. Then someone started clapping, loud and fast, and the idea and its intent spread in an instant. Soon everyone in the room was standing up and cheering and hollering, hoisting their glasses and puffing their chests. Everyone was looking at the open kitchen across the room, looking at Angel Miranda, the man who had reopened his restaurant and our own little part of New Orleans when so much else was empty and abandoned. The dining room was seized by a spontaneous standing ovation. It took Angel a moment, but then he looked up from the fire-licked skillets on his stove and surveyed the situation in his restaurant. He gave a little wave, a shy acknowledgment, and then clapped his hands at his beaming waitresses and implored them to get back to work.

I found Angel a few days later relaxing and watching a Spanish soccer team on television. I asked him about the opening night scene.

"I was so tired from getting the restaurant open," he said. "You know, we had a lot to do with cleaning everything up and finding people to work. I was just so tired I couldn't even show how touching it was when they stood up for me like that. But inside my heart was bulging with happiness."

Our New Orleans was coming back, but so slowly that we had to squint to see it in the distance. We were like shipwreck survivors on a raft who could catch glimpses of an approaching mast on the horizon—but only between the swell and trough of the waves tossing our leaky little craft around.

So our hearts periodically bulged with happiness too. They bulged every time we heard something that sounded like our New Orleans on the radio and every time we saw something that looked like our New Orleans on television. And our hearts bulged every time we ate something that tasted like our New Orleans.

The cities and towns where New Orleans people found themselves stranded after the levee failure offered varying degrees of hospitality, but none of them could provide anything like New Orleans food. These cities could have excellent cuisine, stuff to make food critics swoon, and chefs who could set trends for expensive restaurants all over the world to follow, but it still would not be New Orleans food, the high and low food that wrote "HOME" in big capital letters across our palates. Even in Baton Rouge, just eighty miles upriver, there was nothing that even came close to replicating the food that New Orleans people think of when they think of home.

"What they call a po-boy loaf is like a glorified hotdog bun," said Mike Serio, the owner of a po-boy shop called Mike Serio's Deli downtown near my office. "The first loaf I got my hands on here, the real stuff? It took months to get it and I tore into it like an animal, I ate half the loaf dry, it was so good."

The bread that received such ravaging in Mike Serio's hands was an airy, crisply crusted loaf from Leidenheimer Baking Co., the century-old New Orleans bakery that was able to deliver its first postdiluvian loaves six weeks after the storm. The bakery promptly received letters from residents who wanted to personally thank the owners for getting it back running again so soon.

Everything in New Orleans was suddenly and radically short-staffed, bakeries included, and a lot of equipment necessary for making and moving New Orleans food was destroyed, damaged, or stolen. Most of the Leidenheimer bakery's delivery trucks were commandeered after the flood by people looking for any conveyance out of the city. These trucks are hard to miss. They are approximately the size and shape of a UPS delivery truck, but instead of the trademark brown paint job they are covered in giant images of "Vic and Nat'ly"—a pair of local comic strip characters who resemble the type of overweight, bouffant-coiffed folks found at failing bowling alleys everywhere—plus cartoon renderings of huge po-boys dripping mayonnaise and gravy. Riding out of town in one of these trucks would be like fleeing another city in a rolling, stolen billboard advertising one of that town's peculiar charms. Still, enough bakers were back in New Orleans by October to allow Leidenheimer to reopen, even if the first deliveries to the po-boy shops had to be made in the bakers' own personal cars. They were welcomed with gratitude by other people who were unsure if they would ever eat or sell another po-boy again.

At Guy's Po-Boys way uptown on Magazine Street, owner Marvin Matherne was in despair wondering how he would open his own business without any employees back in the city. He was really at a personal low point, he told me, doubting the future of his business and doubting his crumbled city. It was just another example of that snowball effect after Katrina that hit so many of us, when one added or unexpected difficulty on top of all the others threatened to bring the whole pile of woe down in a crashing tumble. That was when a neighbor walked past Guy's Po-Boys, stopped to talk to Marvin, and volunteered on the spot to help. She left just a week later to take a higher-paying recovery contract job with FEMA, but, before she left, the baton was passed to another neighbor who volunteered to help. Later still, the young daughter of a regular customer took over the shift, answering phones and running the register while Marvin worked a griddle snapping with hot sausage and grilled shrimp for his po-boys.

"This was not a career move for any of the people who helped out here, believe me," he told me one day when he had a slightly more normalized staffing schedule nailed down. "These were neighbors helping me out who wanted to get New Orleans rolling again, and po-boys is New Orleans."

The first restaurants to open, of course, were ones with little or no flood damage. Others were utterly annihilated, including some of the great old neighborhood restaurants around Mid-City.

Two blocks from my house was Mandina's, a Creole restaurant that opened in an old corner grocery just after Prohibition was lifted in 1933. The business had expanded into a collection of small dining rooms added over the generations that followed, and the rooms were always crowded. Old folks piled in early for dinner and after church on Sundays. Men in ties crammed the doorway for weekday lunches. The waiters knew from countless repetition which ones wanted martinis and which ones wanted old fashioned cocktails and would deliver them even before the garlic-smeared French bread arrived. There were neon signs in the windows facing the streetcars on Canal. You could sit in the dining room— wearing a suit or shorts, at your discretion—and drink tea or draft beer while a waiter in a bow tie brought you trout meunière, fried oyster po-boys, shrimp remoulade, and bread pudding with whiskey sauce. When you ordered a bowl of turtle soup, the waiter would produce a large bottle of cheap sherry from a sideboard in the corner and add a liberal pour to the roux.

When the levees failed after Katrina, the floodwater rose high enough inside Mandina's dining room to cover the bar. Walking by one day a few weeks after my return home, I found the doors wide open and a group of men and young boys inside wearing breathing masks and rubber boots. They were busily ripping out all the mold-covered walls and woodwork in the place with hammers and pry bars. They let me in to look around and take pictures. A boy who was about ten years old was sitting on top of the flood-warped bar pouring bottles of scotch and vodka into a trash barrel and tossing the empties into a crate.

"Hey, mister," he called to me. "Come take a picture of this. Bet you'll never see this again! Too young to drink and I'm busting up this bar!"

The boy's father put down the sledgehammer he was using against a wall and walked gingerly across the top of the unsteady bar to join his son as I took their picture.

It would take many months more for any of the deeply flooded restaurants to begin reopening, but when they did their regulars who were back in town lined up greet them. One of the first back in the really badly flooded parts of Mid-City was Betsy's Pancake House, a classic diner on Canal Street with thin coffee, thick stacks of cheap pancakes, and waitresses who address just about everyone as either "hon," "baby" or "dawlin'." Betsy's bucked the sad trend of MIA employees and disappeared friends, and when the diner reopened the same women were there on its first day back in business, taking orders from the same cops and utility workers and retirees who had turned up each morning for years.

"How you want your eggs?" a waitress asked one man among the ceaseless flow of regulars who were greeted with hugs on that first morning back.

"I want them looking at me," he said.

"Okay, so over easy," the waitress said.

"No, no," chimed in a second waitress, overhearing the exchange. "'Looking at me' means sunny side up."

"Yeah, but when he says it he means over easy," the first waitress replied. "It's a good thing I'm here. I know what he wants better than he does. Who fed you while we were closed?"

To watch some of the patrons interacting with their waitresses at Betsy's, it seemed like they hadn't been able to find a decent breakfast since the hurricane hit. One elderly man was even chastised by the cashier for his trimmed-down waistline.

"You got no excuses for losing any more weight, we're back now," the cashier told him, ringing up another four-dollar house special of bacon, pancakes with butter scoops, eggs coated with butter, and grits gilded with still more butter.

Betsy's had plenty to contend with itself during the months it was shuttered. The ground-level building was inundated with sixty-two inches of water after the levees failed.

"And that's a lot, I'm only sixty-one and a half inches tall myself," said owner Betsy McDaniel, who makes every half inch of her stature count as she works her dining room. She runs the place, and she also buses tables, takes orders, brews coffee, and harangues the kitchen through the service window to pick up the pace. But she couldn't do any of those tasks on the big reopening day without stopping to receive a hug from a returning regular.

"You really get to know people when you see them every day," she told me during a pause in the morning rush. "And when you can't see them for a while and you want to, you know you start to miss them like family."

Betsy's was the kind of place where décor meant a collage of stuff tacked to the walls and built up over the years into a sum greater than its parts. All of that was destroyed by the flood, all the old photos and proclamations and thrift store art and newspaper clippings. But some customers decided to help out with the redecorating job by bringing in their own new contributions the day the diner reopened. Someone brought a jar of fava beans, which Italian families in New Orleans tend to regard generally as a good luck charm and specifically as a talisman against starvation. It was placed near the cash register together with a flask of holy water and a prayer card to St. Joseph.

"St. Joseph is the carpenter, you know," Betsy said while inspecting the makeshift shrine on that first morning back. "We needed him around here. We had to rebuild the whole place, and you know we were praying to him. I think that's the only reason I could get this place open again. St. Joseph wanted me to get off his back."

Seven   Ground Scores

Whether it was considered treasure or just plain clutter, most of the stuff in our homes was trash after the levee failure, and all of it ended up on the street. Katrina debris was a collage of broken building materials—the moldy drywall, the rusty pipes, and shattered porcelain—mixed up with belongings that never would have been tossed under normal circumstances. That was the precious stuff, the keepsakes and memorabilia, the photos and trophies and art. And it was joined by the merely valuable, like all the appliances and DVDs and furniture. All of it was soaked and ruined but still distinguishable for its former worth as it lay discarded in the street.

For the more industrious and mechanically adept, the temptation to scavenge was sometimes too much to resist. My friend Todd Windisch, the building contractor, seems able to repair any kind of engine short of a turbojet, and he was convinced he could get half the lawn mowers he saw discarded on the streets running again. His wife, Erin Peacock, made him stop after he had filled their backyard with something like a dozen of them, all flooded and filthy and lined up on the dead grass like a ruined taxi fleet. But he later found a loophole in her embargo when he brought home a huge, expensive-looking stainless steel barbecue grill that worked perfectly fine once he jury-rigged the rusted-out gas valve.

The flooded neighborhoods were literally caked with the randomly distributed contents of other people's lives, and those who might have been mere recyclers before the storm suddenly found themselves elevated to the status of found-object artists as they sorted through it all. Every step through the neighborhoods revealed yet another example of some ruined consumer item or personal belonging that was now an artifact imbued with new, sad meaning in the context of its destruction and loss. It might have been someone's senior year art portfolio or a cheerleading trophy or a relative's letter writ-

88

ten from Weimar Germany or a chicken-scratch shopping list for milk and toilet paper. It didn't matter. A walk down the street became a sortie through an incomparable, ever-changing stack of archival material, all of it firsthand, scarred, and vulnerably naked to the sun, rain, or crunch of the next bulldozer to come along and haul it to buried, crushed oblivion if someone didn't snatch it up.

Todd was hardly the only one with the collector's itch. There was so much around, it actually took an act of restraint to keep from picking up some flooded but fascinating treasure on every trip outside the house. A grand piano will disintegrate into its smaller components after it sits under water for a few weeks, but those fallen pieces still look like they came from a grand piano, and it was tempting to think how impressive that tarnished and bucktoothed keyboard would look displayed over a mantelpiece, like a swordfish trophy at a fishing lodge. Even the scrap lumber—the sawed-off lengths of old southern heart pine floorboards, the broken bits of gingerbread carpentry detailing, the deeply grooved molding, the framing studs cut from ancient swamp cypress so dense that today's nails bounce off them—even when discarded in the filthy street, it could all look beautiful enough to collect and reuse, to elevate and restore to some kind of significance.

But no artist could hope to compete with the masterworks of composition achieved at random by the flood and the emergency efforts to pile up the debris. The heaps of personal and household stuff formed outside of every gutted house. They were like journals of loss left open on the sidewalk, each offering a perverted peep into the lives of the people who had lived there. These glimpses were disjointed and random and just as incomplete and mesmerizing as an accidental view through a neighbor's backlit window on a dark night.

In one such pile on Telemachus Street were the crumpled rotor blades of a broken ceiling fan, the upturned wheels of a baby stroller, the shuffled deck of a spilled record collection, and, draped over it all, a blue air force uniform with a name badge and an impressive-looking row of medals. This was one of those dioramas of chance that stopped me cold, the kind of thing that forced me to stand outside there and stare, breathing through my mouth to dodge the crawling reek from the months-gone contents of someone's sickening refrigerator a few feet away. On another block down Palmyra Street, there was an old metal kitchen cabinet thrown wholly to the curb. In the top drawer that lay open to view, among the steak knives with rusty blades and the plastic packs of take-out ketchup, was a photo of a tall young man in a Christmas sweater hugging a woman who had her hair whipped up in a meticulous, magnificent coif. They were both smiling so hard for the camera and holding each other so tight that anyone seeing it as I did on the street in the empty moonlight would just have to hope they were okay and hanging in there wherever they happened to be now.

It wasn't even necessary to seek out this stuff. Sometimes it literally blew up to my door, like the random collection of detritus I discovered while picking up garbage tangled in the remains of my front garden. I was plucking at the ground in the rapid pace of a highway litter patrol, trying to clear at least my own few square feet of yard, when I noticed the odd conglomeration of items in my hands. There was a faded instruction manual for a 1970s-vintage vacuum cleaner; a returned, rejected check bearing the name of an elderly neighbor and written before the storm to the local supermarket for groceries, stamped "void" on front and back; a student's homework index card with the term "hydrofluoric acid" written on one side and its accompanying periodic chart abbreviation written on the other; and one page torn from a paperback copy of Gustave Flaubert's novel Madame Bovary. Nearby, I also discovered a sheet of crumpled, dirt-caked notebook paper, which I smoothed out, finding the following written in ballpoint pen ink:

Oakland that's my new address now
I can't believe this shit
Oakland muthafuckin' CA
Anyways I'm chillin' at my new skool
Thinking bout the old skool
Damn my beedie went out
Where's my lighter, oh I found it
And I miss all my friends

T Rose, LaLa, Rili, Daddy, Geno, Freddie, Precious, D-Brown
Yeah, all dem, yeah dem my niggas
I'm thinking bout everything we used to do
Big bomb fest damn near every weekend
We got the hoocka, the Fountain
We got mad muthafuckin bongs
Triple bubble glass bongs
Off the neezie
Itty bitty chrome pipes with black resin interior
It'll send ya
Sometimes that shit was so thick it felt like ecstasy
Nights of restless sex, just because it felt good
People everywhere your every spot touched at least once
Upside down, inside out, front side, back side, side side
And then STOP, yes stop, when you
Cum to that point you have to STOP

There was just no telling where this paean of stoner life might have originated. I knew every person on my block, and none of them seemed likely candidates. Really, it could have traveled from anywhere, and I wondered about the dotted line that brought it to my doorstep. Maybe it had been crammed in a notebook in a bedroom one night and forgotten, shoved in a box of garbage after the storm, tossed out on the street from a moldy house, blown out to the road in the dirty breeze, stuck by a gum of mud to the wheel of a passing truck, and brought over here where it slipped free and found its way into my dead garden.

The private stuff was especially remarkable, the stuff that is normally hidden from casual view but was disgorged along with everything else on the curbside inventories of our lives.

My friend Suzie suffered extreme damage to her house, which she had bought just a year earlier. It was a little cottage built in the late 1940s for G.I. Bill veterans and their pregnant wives, and at the time of construction no thought at all had been given to raising the structures above grade. So Suzie's bachelorette pad was inundated with shoulder-high floodwater and every stitch of her belongings inside was ruined. That included her nightstand, and all the little items she stored in it.

The nightstand was on the curb in her great heap of debris when I dropped by one day. Suzie was outside with a girlfriend, and we stood around talking and sweating, looking over this stinking, wet pile of her belongings when she began distractedly yanking at the nightstand's top drawer, probably in the bored fascination of seeing all her stuff mashed into garbage. And when the drawer reluctantly came open, there emerged her big, bad, neon green vibrator and a collection of related intimate goods, all of them marked with the familiar stain of the flood.

We all saw it at the same time, and Suzie laughed sharply at the spectacle. But when the joke was over and she tried to close the drawer, the flood-warped thing would not budge. She tried again to no avail and then started snickering wickedly. There it was, the rude, sexual thing in open view before us and there was no hiding it.

"Oh fuck it," Suzie said to the sky. "I don't give a damn anymore."

She put her hand in a box of flooded clothing, pulled out a cinnamon colored showgirl wig, tossed it down over the open drawer of bright sex toys, and walked away.

The storm laid it all bare, and I suspect an analysis of flood debris would have revealed quite a bit about my neighbors. The sheer quantity of sex-related merchandise in the postdiluvian street was startling. Every pile of debris seemed to offer something titillating. This was private, hidden stuff cast into the open. Yet however stimulating it may have been in the boudoir, it was now down in the dirt and looked as wretched as a vampire caught in sunlight. Porno DVDs were everywhere, with lurid teaser shots of the scenes promised within staring up dead-eyed from the ground. Dirty magazines were spread wide open on the brown grass. A pink vibrator had been crushed into the street a few doors down by the wheels of a passing truck, its pickle body flattened and the batteries squeezed out the back end. For weeks, Dr. Watson and I stepped around it every day on our walks until it finally disappeared. One day, as the dog and I made our morning walk around the block, we came upon a crew of workmen sorting through a garbage bag of women's clothing left on the curb. The guys held negligees and lacy bras up to their soiled hazmat suits, pranced around a bit like toxic tarts in the dirty street, and then convulsed with laughter.

The Amazing Dr. Watson had his own take on the debris. The wretched piles offered wonderfully complex and compelling landscapes of scent for his hyperactive sniffer, and they must have painted a brilliant olfactory gallery for him on every walk around the neighborhood. Sometimes the debris piles were orderly affairs with large pieces of flood-ruined furniture stacked upon each other, and bags and boxes of other trash brought out to the street. More often, though, the materials appeared to have been flung with shovels from the front door, lost items and waste trailing out from the steps to the street. It looked as though these old houses had opened their doors and vomited up chunky streaks on the front gardens and sidewalks.

These piles were never the same from one day to the next. Homeowners and work crews added new debris to them as they cleared through the houses, but even the static, untouched piles evolved each day as they roasted in the sun or were soaked by rainfall. Cardboard boxes filled with stuff—and carefully taped up by someone in an assertion of anal tendencies that transcended even catastrophe— would inevitably split apart after a rain shower to disgorge their contents. Eventually, the waterlogged cabinets and bureaus and armoires arranged on the sidewalks like outdoor living showrooms would also flake to pieces and collapse in front of their former homes.

Disposing of all this loose discard was no tidy job. FEMA contractors worked block by block. Their crews consisted of someone at the end of each block waving orange flags at the sparse local traffic and men with rakes and shovels scraping the street. The heavy work was done by men in small bulldozers, usually Bobcats, and it was their job to break down the debris piles and ferry the contents to trucks waiting a block away. The business end of these machines were fang-lined steel jaws. When deployed in pairs, they would grab and rip apart awkward or tangled loads like two dingoes fighting over the same scrap of kangaroo.

The crews met up somewhere each morning and headed out in platoons. Some mornings, I would see a group of them with their huge pickup trucks in the lot of a destroyed supermarket or parked on the brown grass along Bayou St. John, all the men circled up around a foreman to receive their instructions. Then they would head out toward their worksites in the manner of a funeral procession, moving in a snaking line of slow-rolling cars packed with guys in their hazmat suits and reflective gear, led by two or more Bobcat tractors. All of them would be progressing at a snail's pace dictated by the low gear grind of the tractors, and the cars had their hazard lights flashing as they drove, in the fashion of mourners headed in formation to a burial.

The tractors were pint-sized, but they made up for their small size by creating a great deal of noise and even more of a mess. For each load a machine lifted, a third of the take would invariably land on the street. The machine's iron teeth would come down hard on a pile of debris, grip, lift, even shake it sometimes, and finally haul off with a load. On the way to the dump truck, anything smaller than a fridge was likely to fall from its grip and drop in a shatter of its broken parts to the street. In this way, the household belongings of just about all of my neighbors were broken apart, crushed into the pavement under heavy wheels, scattered and commingled in a mosaic of loss all down the block.

In addition to their shimmering white hazmat suits, each member of these work crews wore breathing masks, rubber boots, rubber gloves, and hard hats. With all the environmental precautions, they looked like they might have been inspecting a chemical weapons plant rather than raking up sweaters and photo albums and kitchen utensils from New Orleans streets. They looked intimidating and somewhat militaristic at first, but eventually I began to think of them as some pestilent version of the merry little Oompah Loomphas, dressed in their strange, lumpy costumes and mechanically going about their daily rounds.

Meanwhile, I left the house for my morning bicycle commute in nothing more protective than slacks and an Oxford shirt. I gave cautious hello waves of my naked hand to these awkward, alien-looking beings and pedaled on to the relative normalcy of downtown, where the shirt-and-tie look had finally overtaken security ID necklaces and pistol holsters as the most common street attire.

But eventually even the clean-up crews became part of the scenery. The violent noise of their work and their Chernobyl-like outfits grew as normal as the flooded porn and crushed sex toys in the streets, as ordinary as cast-off baby strollers and air force uniforms littering a neighborhood without people.

Not everything tossed to the street was ruined, however. People chucked just about anything in their haste to clean out a damaged house, especially in the early days when the sundown curfew put a tight deadline on a day's work, and commercially viable wares were often caught up in the purge. That's how Todd got his stainless steel barbecue grill, after all, and plenty of other people brought in an ersatz inheritance of barely damaged furniture, strange artwork, and small appliances.

I had been availing myself of ground score bounties like this for a long time before the flood. Back in Rhode Island, there was a seasonal cottage industry that relied entirely on the procuring and reselling of the furniture of rich undergrads at Brown University and the Rhode Island School of Design who found it easier to pitch their belongings to the sidewalk at semester end rather than pack and move it all. There were futons, bookshelves, posters of black and white Parisian street scenes, endless numbers of floor lamps, and sometimes what looked like entire pages of the Ikea catalogue materialized on the sidewalk and free for the taking. Someone with a pickup truck, a worthy back, and a sense of timing could enjoy profitable collection rides around the privileged campuses.

In New Orleans, the Katrina flood brought the richest harvest of ground scores anyone had ever seen. The streets offered up perfectly good bikes, irreplaceable cypress mantelpieces, computer printers, TVs, hat stands, electric organs, antique window frames, Vespa scooters, drum sets, architectural columns, pirogue-style canoes, century-old floor planks, naked and decapitated mannequins, Indian headdresses, and countless other objects. Some were lost causes, some needed a makeover, some just a simple wipe down, and others, inexplicably, no attention at all.

The best thing I ever took from this street harvest, though, was a little dog who scared me so badly the first time I saw her I thought we would have to fight.

Despite the zealous efforts of animal rescue volunteers, there were still many stray and abandoned dogs roaming the streets months after the flood. I had been wary of even the smallest stray ever since that snarling pack had chased me on my bike on Halloween night. My paranoia reached its peak one evening while I was bicycling through the neighborhood around sunset. I heard a sharp, pronounced growl that seemed to be emanating from just outside my peripheral vision, somewhere by the abandoned house I was just passing. It was a slow, deliberate sound that promised bared teeth and bristled fur. My body stiffened instantly and the fear ran through my brain again like blood. But the intensity lasted just a moment. I looked over in mid-pedal to see that the "growling" was actually coming from the teeth of a cordless saw biting slowly through a wooden plank in the hands of a carpenter. He was working by the last minutes of sunlight on the sidewalk outside the house, and he looked up from his job to see me coasting past with a tense face of fearful, flinching anticipation. I might have been embarrassed if I weren't just plain relieved that a huge dog was not about to lunge at me.

Unbitten, I was nonetheless twice shy on the matter of stray dogs roaming my desolate neighborhood. There were nights when I would walk Dr. Watson around the blocks and catch sight of a canine form hunkered low a few yard-lengths ahead of us. I would respond by shifting our course down another street, or if the dog shape ahead was already too close I looked for something hard or sharp among the debris on the ground to use as a weapon. Soon, I began carrying a machete on our walks. I had the thing as a backyard tool to keep the luxuriously fecund banana trees at bay. But I grabbed it one night as Dr. Watson and I stood at the threshold of the blackened house about to embark on a walk through the darkness outside. It became standard equipment for a while on each of the strange, nervous tours around the neighborhood.

It was all a little much. Nothing worse than a few legitimate growls ever came my way after that Halloween chase, and here I was arming myself for some kind of man-vs.-beast confrontation. But by this point I was well under the wicked spell of my surroundings, and the worst seemed entirely plausible. I had literally grown afraid of the dark. On the worst nights, I watched from my porch as the haunted, wet sunsets bled through the barren limbs of dead magnolia trees across the street, the last rays of light seeming like the final grains of a portentous hourglass dribbling out. And when the Transylvanian dark was complete, the scared, twitchy bands of stray dogs slinking around out there were transformed in my mind to the specter of wolf packs prowling this godforsaken landscape. When the sun went down, I always knew where the lanterns were and I always had a machete close by.

It was in this wounded state of mind that I first encountered Ginger. The first sighting occurred while I was lying on my back under the house, using a garden sprayer to blast bleach at the little reefs of green and white mildew that had formed in the moist darkness there after the flood. I was resting a bit in the close, underhouse quarters, feeling claustrophobic and a little sorry for myself in the mud, rubbing my bleach-stung eyes. I heard something move nearby and my eyes snapped open. I saw a dog walking slowly beneath the house about a room length away from me. She looked to be about forty or fifty pounds. She was muttly and was covered in dirty bluish fur. Her tail was tucked between her legs protectively, and her rear end had knocked against some shredded bit of air conditioning ductwork left dangling from the floorboards above. I gripped the trigger of the bleach-filled garden sprayer and thought I might use it against the dog's face if she charged at me. But the dog didn't seem to notice me, and in a moment she passed coolly out from underneath my house and disappeared beneath my neighbor's house. I started breathing again, then crawled stiffly out from under the house to see where the dog had gone, but there was no sign of her.

Later on, as I got to know the dog, I learned that she would traverse entire blocks using the crawlspaces beneath our houses as her own subway system, exposing herself to view only in the narrow alleys between the buildings or when she darted out to grab food left in the open.

The dog was no doubt terrified, but at least she was not going hungry. There was no lack of dog food around the neighborhood. Animal rescue volunteers were everywhere, and they seemed at times to be working at cross-purposes. Some dropped huge caches of pet food on porches and street corners to keep animals fed and self-sufficient, while others tried to lure hungry animals into humane traps to get them to shelters.

The city became a destination for animal causes, and volunteers flocked here from everywhere. They saved countless animals that had been abandoned by their owners and often went to heroic measures to do so—boating through flooded blocks, risking the snapping jaws of traumatized dogs, scaling trellises to pluck petrified cats from teetering balconies. But before long their more extreme rescue efforts began to run afoul of the delicate sense of normalcy the returning residents were trying to knit together in their neighborhoods.

Todd and Erin had a confrontation through the bars of their locked gate with a patrol of rescuers who demanded they turn over their dog. The rescuers told them they had orders from the Louisiana governor herself to collect any dog they saw. They had seen Todd and Erin's dog lounging on their porch behind the gate, which constituted probable cause. Todd made sure they left without the dog, governor's orders notwithstanding. A story spread about another man who came home from a trip to gather ice from the Red Cross station across town to discover that his dogs had been taken from his fenced yard. He later found them at a collection point for rescued animals. And there was the often-repeated story of the couple who sat down to an MRE dinner by candlelight in their boarded-up house just moments before the door was kicked in by the boots of animal rescuers who heard a dog barking protectively at them from inside.

I was walking the Amazing Dr. Watson around my block one afternoon when I encountered an animal rescue volunteer patrolling the street.

"That dog must be yours, right?" she called out to me from a few house lengths away.

"That's right," I said. "That's why he's walking with me on this leash."

"Well, that's good. We're looking for strays. There's one down here I've been trying to get for hours."

I looked down the nearby alley and saw the same small, bluish ghost of a dog that had given me such a scare under my house. The dog was standing very still and staring back at us. She could not have looked less fierce standing there in the sun, her tail between her legs again, her ears down and her bearing just generally pathetic. The woman made a move for her, and the dog instantly dashed under the house and out of sight.

"It's been like this. I've even crawled underneath houses for her, but she won't let me get near her," the woman said.

Another woman driving a pickup truck pulled into the intersection just ahead. "Are you okay?" she called from the truck, talking to the other woman but motioning her head towards me.

"Yeah, don't worry, he's okay," she answered.

"Well, I saw another one down here, let's go get him," the driver said.

"Maybe we'll get this one later," the woman said, looking down the empty driveway where the little dog had been. "Make sure you keep your dog on a leash, okay?"

I saw the same dog a few days later, peering at me from an alleyway a few doors down from my house as I took Dr. Watson on his morning walk. She seemed inquisitive, twitching her nose at Dr. Watson and at me in what looked like a fidgety effort to sniff us without getting too close. There was no way to be scared of her now. When I took a step toward her she slipped back underneath the house.

The very next day I saw her again, and the scene went down in just the same way, as it did the day after that and the next one after that. But each morning it seemed that I could get a little closer. She was clearly a mutt, and after a few of these sightings I began to piece together her lineage. She had the body size and shape of a pit bull and a face somewhat like a Labrador retriever. Her fur was coarse, her tongue had black marks on it, and she trailed off in a little rat-tail. So, in essence, she was a standard New Orleans street dog. She had no tags or even a collar, but was liberally spotted with patches of callused skin where her fur was stripped away. In the moments before she scuttled back to the darkness of whatever house she was camping under, her nervous eyes and shuffling nose seemed nothing less than imploring. It was like she wanted to follow us home, but was too frightened to get close.

I didn't want a second dog, though before the storm I had made a few attempts to get one. There was Boris, the regally fluffy golden retriever given away by a local Russian woman on the heels of a divorce. I technically did adopt him but had to return the dog a week later after balking at the previous owner's insistence that I allow her unlimited visitation rights. Then there was the pit bull mix who guarded the used car lot near my house, who looked like a scrapper from across the street but who responded so ebulliently when I passed close with my own dog—his tail wagging with frenzy, his nose shoved through the chain link, and his tongue coming through to lick Dr. Watson's face when we drew right up to the fence—that it was impossible to feel anything but pity for his lonely life on duty. Sometimes I packed a few biscuits in my pocket when I took Dr. Watson out on his evening walk just so I could slip them through the fence to the guard dog, who took them from my fingers very delicately. When I found him running loose a few blocks away one morning, collarless and excited, I got right next to him and considered bringing him home. But then a guy from the car lot pedaled by on his bike, screamed at the dog and chased it back, scurrying, to his fence line. I never saw that dog after Katrina, though I could spot his sad little doghouse at the back of the destroyed car lot whenever I walked past, and it looked just as ravaged and flood-stained as any of the people's houses around it.

So while I really did not want to add the rehabilitation of someone else's pet to my docket of recovery projects, seeing this little abandoned dog every morning got to me. I thought about her sleeping underneath an empty house in an empty neighborhood on my block all winter long by herself. I was sleeping upstairs and had my own dog for company and it was bad enough.

One day I decided to go after her. I used Dr. Watson as bait, tying him to a fence post by the house where we usually found the stray and threading a trail of dog biscuits from the alley to the perimeter of Watson's leash length, just out of his reach. The stray emerged from beneath the house and followed the biscuit trail. She looked at Watson, looked at me, looked back at Watson, and kept eating. I lunged for her, and she evaded me easily and scurried under the house. I reset the biscuit bait, and we did the same dance again, but on this second attempt I caught her. I held her down and stroked her at the same time, and I knew in a second she wouldn't try to bite me. Meanwhile, Dr. Watson was beside himself, doing an agitated tap dance with his front two paws and straining his leash while his tail wagged furiously behind him. Holding the stray down, I managed to take the leash off Watson and put it on her. I took my weight off her and she shot to her feet, but the moment she felt the leash tug at her neck she stopped struggling. It was as though she understood that she was back under human care. She stood still and looked up at me as Watson gave her a thorough going-over with his snorting snout.

I thought I would name her Slate in honor of her blue-gray coloring. But as I gave her a first bath with the garden hose, the dirt and grime washed off, and the color of her coat changed to burnt caramel flecked with strange, black wicks, almost like bristles. So while she was still dripping wet, her new name changed to Ginger.

I took Ginger to the neighborhood vet over by Bayou St. John. She was fully degreed and licensed but nonetheless ran her practice even before the storm as a sort of speakeasy animal clinic. She cared for her neighbors' pets in the ground floor of a huge old Creole townhouse with no visible business signs, and she posted no ads. She got all her clients through referrals, and the low profile might have been the reason her clinic wasn't sacked for pills by drug-addict looters after the storm. She gave Ginger a regimen of shots and medication and advised me that the welts and scars and callous scrub marks all over her body predated the storm and were probably the result of prolonged, habitual abuse.

This explained a lot, especially combined with whatever she had been through during the storm and the last three months of its aftermath. Even after we cleaned her up, Ginger was a mess. Her normal posture was one of preemptive cowering, her head bowed and her back to a wall, and for no apparent reason at all she would start trembling like a light aircraft in heavy turbulence. Any loud or hard noise sent her diving for the floor.

When I returned home from work in the evenings, she would join Dr. Watson as he ran up to greet me at the door, but a moment later she would scurry off, looking for cover. Her preferred hiding spot in my house was under the bed. But she also had a tendency to leap onto my bed and pee on it. With no viable laundry facility anywhere nearby after the storm, this presented a big problem. The cold nights I had to sleep on the floor after cleaning Ginger's pee off my own bed marked low points in dog-owner relations in my household. Even Dr. Watson looked guilty and apologetic on those nights, as if embarrassed for the behavior of one of his species.

I closed off my room to her, but Ginger quickly found other places to hide. This was impressive considering that the downstairs rooms were partially gutted at this point and had no furniture besides folding chairs and a workbench. One night, she hid herself away particularly well, and I had to search each room of the dark house several times with a flashlight before finally catching the glint of her eyes looking nervously out at me from the back of a halfway demolished kitchen cabinet.

I have tried to decode Ginger's behavior ever since I took her in, but it is incredibly disjointed. When she is nervous, which is most of the time, her face gets tight and her eyes bulge and dart around like a bat. In repose, she often lies on her side with her legs sticking out across the floor and looks a lot like a pot-bellied pig. When she sniffs the breeze with that deep contemplative air of olfactory study, she looks like a horse, and she sounds like a horse whinnying when she gives a heavy nasal exhale. Other times, her jowls puff out and in quickly like a croaking toad. Her strangely spiky coat is like a badger's, her tail like a rat's, and she is twitchy like a bird. In short, Ginger is a freaky little dog with an identity problem. But somehow, as the months crunched by in the dark of my weird neighborhood and as my mind stewed in the murk, she seemed like the perfect mascot for the absurd, deserted calamity all around us.

Eight   Open Houses

When I first started trying to buy my own house, before I met Mrs. Minnette and saw the house I would fall in love with, the most intriguing part of the whole real estate process was touring through properties put up for sale. The upper limit of my price range was very low, so most of the places I saw were old New Orleans shotgun houses that had been cut into any number of shoddy apartments over the years by distant landlords. It always seemed that the houses my real estate agent and I visited were still occupied by tenants during our inspections, and quite often the landlord had not told them in advance about our visit or even that the property was for sale.

An extended family would be there, sitting silently around a kitchen table or all jammed together on a couch in front of the TV, with kids and nieces and young in-laws all watching us and all of them very clearly under the threat of a devastating ass-whooping from the head of the household should they break decorum. The agent and I would walk through, and I would wave a small, awkward hello greeting to the clustered family watching us, and we would proceed to tap our heels on floorboards, eyeball the extent of termite damage and, in the relative privacy of a bathroom or crooked hallway, discuss the big, round-numbered estimates for what it might take to fix the place up. We walked through their rooms—past the stationary exercise bike in one room and the poster of the teenage heartthrob tacked to the wall of the next and the pot of boiling spaghetti in the kitchen. The voyeur in me couldn't get enough of it. Sometimes the agent and I would pull up outside a house that I instantly knew I wouldn't buy—be it too ugly, too new, or situated on a block too thickly infested with thugs—but still I would insist on taking the tour solely for the chance to poke through the rooms and hallways and peer out their windows at the street and yard, to see their lives and their things.

After Katrina, half the properties around my neighborhood were unintended open houses, and my nightly walks with the two dogs provided boundless opportunities for self-guided tours. The houses were not only empty of people; they were literally wide open. Doors had been knocked in by rescue workers and left swinging on their hinges. In many cases, it was possible to stand on the sidewalk, look in the front door of a house, and see clear to the back through room after empty room.

Sometimes exterior walls were completely ripped off, leaving nothing to cover a home's ground level besides structural studs and window frames hanging there, lost-looking and suspended in the space where siding and plaster had once made a room. They were like concept houses or design renderings with the walls erased to show the floor plan within. If these houses had brochures—some type of twisted, poststorm marketing material—the copywriter could brag on the wonderful opportunity to configure the rooms to suit a buyer's own personal lifestyle. Put the walls wherever you like! Swap the kitchen with the front bedroom! It's a blank slate! What options!

Sometimes I went inside these open houses. The excursions were unspeakably creepy and, technically speaking, an act of trespassing. It occurred to me occasionally that a National Guard patrol might take me for a late-blooming looter. But I wasn't interested in stealing anything. Rather, these open houses were like invitations to explore my new habitat, as if they were all just a part of my natural range in this vile landscape. What was unthinkable in normal days—barging into someone's home uninvited—seemed totally acceptable in the abandoned moonlight of empty blocks. Curiosity put a hook in my nose and tugged me in.

I rarely used the doors. More often, I would pass the flank of a corner house, notice a missing wall, look the place up and down, and then step up and inside through the wide gap between studs where the siding, insulation, and drywall had been. When the dogs were with me I assisted their leaps up after me with the kind of motion you use to pull a dog into the bed of a pickup truck. Then we would stand there in the erstwhile home, surveying spaces where only a few surviving details suggested their former lives as particular types of rooms. A square of bleach-scalded floorboard, a rectangle of molded floorboard—it was hard to tell the difference without the context of walls and furniture. But in one space there might still be a chandelier hanging from the remains of the ceiling. That meant a living room or maybe a dining room. If another space had a few sawed-off pipes jutting up from the floor, that was probably the kitchen.

The dogs wandered at will from space to space, but I developed a little obsession with finding the dead center of a building. These are often obscure spots, it turns out, and under normal circumstances there is often no way to actually stand on one. I usually had to pass through the frames of missing walls to get there, brushing past the chalky remains of gutted plaster. Sometimes I found the spots right beneath staircases or bull's-eyed by decayed holes in pine floorboards where concealed pipes had rusted and leaked for years behind walls. But that was the destination of my new little mania, tracking down the architectural gravity at the heart of these old structures now that they were so open and stripped out. I would simply stand there for a bit, focusing my imagination on what the place might have been like when it was filled with people, when it was a house resonating with footfalls and squeaks and sneezes and heartbeats.

Other houses weren't empty. These were the houses where no one had made it back to clean them out, and they sat like time capsules to the moment when their inhabitants left, though of course they were growing progressively more moldy and rank as the unattended months marched on.

This was the case for a house just down the block from mine. The glass in the front door was shattered, and the screen door would swing open at the wind's discretion, presenting a jagged frame for the view into the first few rooms I began to think of it as the Katrina Museum, and although it was a static exhibit, I still checked in every few days when walking past with the dogs. The curator of chance had created a truly engaging exhibit, expertly presenting artifacts to evoke questions and suggest the details of the life once lived here. The pillows and blankets arranged on the now-moldy couch seemed to indicate that someone had been lying there prior to evacuation, maybe curled up near the door with an ear open for looters. There was a movie poster on the wall showing Chuck Norris with a pair of submachine guns, and he stared across the room at a framed print of a pair of dolphins swimming under a rainbow. The dining room table was set for three people, with a glass vase in the center still holding the stems of dead flowers. The television was enormous, and the doors of the cabinet on which it sat had flaked open from the water to reveal a collection of children's videos stacked up within, molded together now into one piece.

And the killer detail on the whole vignette, the curator's finest stroke, was a collection of Heineken beer bottles, a dozen or so all full and still capped, standing on the coffee table and on a stereo speaker and even on the windowsill, distributed around the living room for some reason that remained mysterious to me.

I could see these green bottles even from the street sometimes when I passed the house's compromised front door. Whenever I caught sight of them, I thought of my friend Keith Hurtt and his unshakeable faith that flooded beers were perfectly good as long as their seals were intact. Bar owners had thrown out case after case of inventory as they emptied their flooded businesses, and Keith thought nothing of salvaging these discarded beers whenever he saw them on the sidewalk. He was especially keen for Dixie longnecks, the beer produced just a few blocks away from our houses in a towering, industrial-age fortress of a brewery in big tanks made from Louisiana swamp cypress. The brewery had been flooded like just about everything else around it, and the future of the old Dixie brand was in doubt. So each bottle Keith found was a consumable, intoxicating artifact of prestorm New Orleans and, to his eyes at least, they were left out for the taking in their sodden cardboard cases like flooded Easter egg baskets.

"I wash off the bottles and they're good to go," he told me. "If that little cap kept the beer in, it must keep the water out. So what's the difference?"

I couldn't come up with an answer, but I also never drank one with him. Still, Keith managed to harvest a stash of free beer from the streets that lasted him until the first corner stores downtown started selling fresh inventory again.

I spent a lot of my evenings after work walking the neighborhood. The dogs were part of the reason, but also there was very little else to do on the home front at night. Monks might have found inspiration in the quiet, undistracted solitude of my sometimes temperate, but increasingly freezing house and its fathomless neighborhood. But I was restless.

Dinner at home was truly a quick affair with no gas or electricity. Food prep was a simple matter of opening this or that can of beans and tomatoes, combining them with liberal doses of Crystal hot pepper sauce and Creole seasoning and wolfing it all down along with a can of beer plucked from the tepid cooler. That took care of approximately ten minutes. Feeding the dogs consumed about sixty seconds from the moment I pulled out the bag of kibble to the point when both dogs were licking the edges of each other's bowls, unwilling to believe without evidence that one had completely finished before the other.

And that wrapped up domestic duties. Trying to accomplish any serious house repairs by candlelight after a day working downtown proved futile. Just trying to sweep the floor in the partial dark seemed pointless and beyond pathetic. So I took to walking the streets simply for something to do.

For an empty neighborhood, there was sometimes quite a bit to see around Mid-City. The clear starry sky was lovely, though it was impossible to forget that the astral lightshow seemed so bright only because there was no competing illumination around in this once glowing city. But other times, when the moon was up and the wind was blowing in the clouds, the night sky was like a moving mural of tides. It seemed to put the whole world in motion.

On nights like this, my footsteps and the pace of the dogs walking with me and the sizeless amber clouds above all seemed in synch. It took only a small leap of imagination to feel the infinitesimal spin of the globe under my feet as well. It was a helpful exercise in perspective. If I looked down it would be trash and debris and rot and waste. If I looked to the side it was crumbled houses and ruined stores, wrecked cars, and mountains of garbage. But when I looked up it was the lace of oak limbs raking their branches through the clouds. And those clouds were being pushed through the sky by the same wind blowing over the cups of my ears, activating the blood and lighting up my senses.

There were plenty of pitfalls waiting for a sensitive heart in this shattered landscape, though, from picturing the whole area under-water to simply thinking about the family that had lived at this or that particular house along a ruined block and wondering where they possibly could be now. Some type of self-directed distraction was crucial to rein in this kind of brooding, but it wasn't easy. I thought carrying my battery-powered radio on the walks to listen to WWOZ would help. But the station's signal was still tenuous, and, when it cut out, those prolonged gaps of dead air echoed in the si-lent night as yet another totem of the city's crippled condition.

It wasn't long before I set the radio aside and began making my own music for the walks. This started out like singing in the shower, just random bits of lyrics from a mishmash of half-remembered songs that trailed off mid-chorus or were transformed into atonal scatting when I forgot the words. I chopped up and rearranged various blues standards, show tunes, and pop songs and came up with my own parodies. Elton John's "Candle in the Wind" became, in my own al fresco songbook, something I called "Candles and Some Gin," a nod to two pillars of support in the present conditions. Bob Dylan's "Like a Rolling Stone" became "Like a Flooded Home," and even "What Shall We Do With the Drunken Sailor" turned into "What Shall We Do With the Broken Levees" (one answer was "fill the breaches with politicians, early in the morning," though there were many others).

What my singing exercise lacked in musical beauty, it made up for in volume. If anyone else was around, they could have heard me coming from a block away. I walked down the middle of the street, looked up at the dark windows of the empty houses, and sang right at them, like a rough serenade to bashful ghosts hiding somewhere up there. No matter what I sang, it always felt like a huge morale boost and put a little pep in my stride. Even the dogs seemed to walk faster when I was singing, though I suppose it's possible they were just trying to get their ears farther from my mouth.

I often had no itinerary for these trips, and the dogs and I would simply walk around the streets or along the motionless bayou for a few hours. Other times we would walk to one of the handful of bars that had reopened, like the candlelit Banks Street Bar or the places about a mile away in Faubourg St. John that hadn't flooded very deeply and had electricity back. One of those destinations was Pal's Lounge. Like Finn McCool's, the pub over by my house, Pal's had been essentially an alcoholics' maintenance bar for a long time until new owners took over and shook things up a few years before the storm. It was a narrow space in a small building that looked like it might have been a corner store some generations back. The new owners brought in a whole different crowd and a fresh sheen of style that ran toward tattoo-tough and pinup girl–cool. If Finn McCool's could have the warmth of a family reunion at an Irish country pub, Pal's Lounge was like sneaking out to a rock concert with your rebellious older cousin.

Despite the hipster vibe, though, Pal's was still a New Orleans neighborhood bar, and that meant its regulars used it as their community clubhouse. The place was considered "dog friendly," and Dr. Watson knew from his many visits just where to sit by the end of the bar to best focus his stare and remind the bartender that there was a jar of biscuits stashed on the liquor shelf. Jo Starnes, one of the bartenders, was also a hair stylist, and on her nights off from pouring drinks she would give cheap haircuts to shaggy patrons in the corner of the room by the dartboard. One night a week, my friend Erin Peacock set up a table near the big picture window, with nail polish and files and various other beauty products, and offered a package deal called the "manicure and martini special" for some bargain price. George, an instructor at a local culinary training program who was approaching retirement age, would at least once a week bring in some vat of gumbo or jambalaya or a tray of barbecued chicken that he laid out on the bar for everyone to eat for free.

Naturally, when Pal's reopened that autumn, its regulars who had made it back to the city by then soon turned up at its door. Some of them were gutting their homes or had been kicked out of their apartments and were living miles away in FEMA trailers or with relatives or in motel rooms. But they still came over to Pal's to meet up with anyone else who might be back and check out the bar's post-Katrina condition. Even months after the storm, people still had a sense of wonder that some of their favorite New Orleans places were still standing and open again.

Pal's took on a bit of water from the flood, but emerged in such solid condition that even the 1970s vintage *Playboy* centerfolds plastering the men's room wall were intact. Still, the place was marked by the unshakeable shadow of Katrina in a way that ran deeper than structural damage or flood lines. It was something dark and worried that the bartenders and the patrons and even the patrons' dogs brought in with them from the streets. We were all tense and jumpy and raw, and it rubbed off everywhere we went, even when we were trying to relax and kick back in the old happy places.

One night while I was at Pal's the electricity cut off, just one of the many periodic power failures that continued to plague the areas where nominal utility service had been restored. Immediately, the mood changed from the normal, low-level worry to utter panic. There were a half dozen people in the bar, and we all helped the bartender light candles quickly, but she was convinced Katrina-like looting and criminal rampages would sweep through the area at any moment. She brought out a baseball bat, laid it on top of the bar at the ready, and ran up front to bolt the door shut. There was nothing doing outside, where a blackout of the handful of houses actually occupied again didn't really change the neighborhood's appearance much. A National Guard Humvee cruised past on its normal patrol. Eventually the bartender relaxed a bit and served us all another round, though she kept the door bolted.

New Orleans businesses were trying to keep a fragile sense of order aloft just as the damaged households were, but it wasn't always possible. We were all subject to the weird, oppressive environment around us. People walked into Pal's on any given night with something like shell shock written on their faces after a drive through the neighborhood. Even if they arrived with friends, they usually had to sit there at the bar and finish a drink or two in silence before they really started talking or relaxing, as if they had to thaw out a bit in the familiar lights and glow of Pal's after their wasteland journey.

I showed up one night after a long, dark walk holding the dogs' two leashes in one hand and an oil lantern in the other. I noticed Linda, one of Pal's owners, giving me a long, curious look from behind the bar.

"What?" I asked her. "Can't we bring dogs in anymore?"

"Of course you can," she said. "But what is that in your belt? Is that a sword?"

It only then occurred to me that the machete I still carried around sometimes on my nighttime walks—and had on this night tucked into my belt in lieu of a free hand—might not be an appropriate accoutrement for social visits.

"Oh yeah, ah, never mind that," I muttered, embarrassed. It seemed so silly all of a sudden. I ducked outside and hid the big metal blade under some debris, then went back in, sat at the bar, and tried to make jokes about my lingering paranoid fantasies of marauding dog packs out there by the dark bayou.

Of all the exhibits of wasted devastation in my neighborhood, one of the most tortured examples was a big steel warehouse previously used as a distribution center by the *Times-Picayune* newspaper. I passed by the building all the time before the storm. Its big cargo doors were usually open, letting in air and also a view to a multitude of wooden worktables stacked with pillars of folded newspapers all waiting to be delivered around the city. Besides being flooded with six feet of water, the building had also been creamed by the storm winds. One whole corner of the wall was peeled away like the wrapper off a can, and a good piece of the building's roof was bent back to expose the big framing girders underneath. The wind had a way of coming up each time I walked past it, and the structure seemed to broadcast a gut-wrenching cacophony through all its battered pieces. Huge runs of metal siding had come loose, and the wind sucked them out in deep breaths and blew them back against the girders with great crashing noise. The shredded roof hung in sheets from the girders and banged furiously in any wind at all. Long fixtures for fluorescent lights dangled from the rafters, looking like hanged men swinging from on high. The wind put the blades on big metal fans around the space into frantic motion and they scraped their warped wire enclosures like trapped animals. It sounded like fifty men were battering the building to pieces, or like the entire structure was one great, groaning mechanical beast in its death throes.

Walking past this thing was unsettling. It didn't help that it faced the rear loading dock of a Sav-A-Center supermarket and the truck-loads of decaying grocery filth that had been pulled from the store's innards and piled all around. The noise, the stench, the emptiness—it was a big motivation to keep moving. But there was something about it that mesmerized. I could have changed the dog walk route, but I stuck to this block night after night because this morbid mobile of swinging, clanging debris was exceptional. It stood out even in the neighborhood's new, otherworldly landscape where everything was altered and weird.

The same old open house curiosity drew me inside the place one night. By this time, a clean-up crew had been through it, and the vast, gray concrete floor was barren. It was a bright, moonlit night, and the sad, reflected rays beamed into the building through segments of missing roof. I had the dogs with me, and they were uneasy with all the banging, clanging, and scraping noises coming from sources they couldn't see or smell. I peered at the shadows across the huge room for any signs of stray dogs or other threats and saw none. We walked inside, and the dogs kept their ears pricked up while I stood looking through the roof at the passing clouds.

It felt like I was in one of those empty, gutted houses again, like I was standing at its heart and rebuilding its walls and people and stories in my mind. The place was empty and the air was groaning with the noise of wrecked forms, but I felt that the imprint of all the human activity that had gone on here for so long before the storm still seeped through. This was a building where men and women had clocked in early to sort and stack heavy loads of newspapers and had ended up with sore backs and sweaty socks. I spotted a flooded Pepsi vending machine in a corner and thought about the workers taking their breaks around it. The remains of a bathroom were visible nearby, and I imagined someone savoring secret, four-minute naps in there with his head pressed against the wall, which was now missing. These were the slim bits of evidence that life had happened here, but my mind was so arid and thirsty now for the color of the old life and the normal pace of day-to-day bullshit that I had practically made a fetish of its memory.

The building could make all the sounds it wanted, I decided. It was just singing and hollering, and I was making plenty of noise of my own these days, singing my made-up songs in the streets and hollering my inchoate threats and curses to the invisible hands that had spun our city to such a wrong turn. I walked out of the battered building feeling like I had just paid a visit to a troublesome neighbor and learned that we had something in common after all.

Nine Tropical Lows

Nothing in New Orleans was remotely normal that winter, yet at the bank office my workday had settled into a familiar rhythm. There were phone calls and e-mails, coffee breaks and conference calls, consultants and customers and spreadsheets. All we talked about between times was Katrina and whatever we imagined for the future, and most of the business we were doing was somehow stamped with the flood's impact, but it was still a day at work in a functional, wired office with lights and nice people wearing business outfits.

The morning bike ride to work was usually sunny, and, apart from the absence of virtually any other traffic on the six lanes of wide, wide Canal Street, it could feel like any other trip downtown. I learned to look past the liquid remains of the dead dog in its terrible plastic kennel, and eventually someone did remove it. The ruined houses and offices that lined the street on the way downtown had already become too commonplace to notice.

The trip back home after work was something else, though. The winter sunset came down before I left the office, so it was dark on the road when I made it out for the day. The downtown blocks had some activity, and there were streetlights shining even in front of the boarded-up hotels and theaters. But the more I pedaled toward home, the darker it all grew. The downtown lights dissolved behind me, and ahead were the sprawling miles, the blacked-out and desolate grid that stretched on down every side street I pedaled past. I had plenty of warning about the occasional passing car. I could hear the grinding of diesel truck engines from blocks away, and their headlights played on the reflective street signs in front of me as brightly as flashlight beams in a dark room.

The homeward bound commute each night felt like an expedition into the ruins. All the contractors and laborers who had been hammering away in the area during the day would be long gone by the time I left work, and once again there would be no sign of anyone besides the glow of a candle burning in a second-floor window here or there. Mid-City was a bad place to be, and my own feet brought me deeper into it with every turn of the pedals.

Every few nights, a police patrol or the National Guard would spot me on my bike, swerve around and pull me over, demanding an explanation for why I might be venturing this way. Even when it was well before curfew, the police and soldiers never believed I was just innocently heading home from work until they saw the address on my driver's license.

"No shit?" a policeman said one evening while fingering my ID. "Well, good luck up there."

Before long, I came to regard the dark not just as a phase of the day but as its own physical presence. I felt invisible in it and swallowed up by it. It might have been different if I were riding home in a car with the radio on and the glow of the dashboard and the headlights marking the road before me. But I stubbornly insisted on commuting by bicycle, just as I had before the storm. Pedaling home, I would look ahead and see nothing but the blue-black shapes of dark buildings in front and hear just the huffing of my own breath and the whirl of my tires on the street. I imagined how the area would look from above, maybe on some aerial survey of Mid-City, and I knew there would be no visible sign of me pedaling past the ruined high school and the flooded beauty parlor and the gutted McDonald's restaurant with its crusted and broken playground.

It was a drenching, inky darkness that came around as a nightly flood. It crept over rooftops and trees and penetrated windows and filled my eyes and head with its empty presence. It felt primordial. More than once on the bike ride back to the house I knew was waiting somewhere ahead in the dark, I thought about how nightfall must have chased our evolutionary ancestors back to their dugouts and caves to curl up and wonder if the light would emerge again.

When I came to my street I would point my handlebars left, turn off Canal and disappear even from the chance view of a passing car or an army Humvee. My block had absolutely no sign of life as I approached. My house was just another dark and boarded-up façade along one vacant block among thousands of others across the city's flood-ravaged zone.

And finally I would stand before my door, my own portal inside this endless honeycomb of ruined living. I would open the door and discover once again that the dark ink from outside had already beaten me home. The dogs would emerge from their hiding spots under the workbench or in the remains of the kitchen cabinets to nuzzle me a bit as I maneuvered the bicycle through the front room, but even they were barely visible.

The clop of my shoes on the wood floors and the skittering of the dogs' paws would be the only noise across the cold house. My fingers would find the stash of matches I kept on the mantle. The matchbooks were relics from hipster bars and expensive restaurants, most of them still closed from the storm. I would fire up lanterns and candles, and the light they cast became the perimeters of reality in my house. I would hold a lantern ahead of me and plunge from room to room. I never found anything amiss, but nevertheless I always proceeded with caution as the lantern revealed one footstep at a time through the place.

I wondered what I looked like making these rounds. I suppose it wasn't much of a show, just a silent figure walking in the dark, sitting in dark rooms, touching worried dogs, sliding into a dark bed. Sometimes, when I shut a day down and resigned to sleep, I concentrated on my own heartbeat inside my chest, and sometimes I swear I could hear it in the quiet house.

The cold is New Orleans's little surprise for those unfamiliar with the seasons of the subtropics. Certainly, when I first arrived here I assumed the city stayed hot or at least very warm through the year. Palm trees, those international signs of tropical climes, are everywhere in the city. Most houses are built for warm weather, with high ceilings and plenty of ventilation. But I learned in my first full year in New Orleans that it not only gets cold but can get much colder than the numbers on the thermometer would suggest, thanks to the area's championship-grade humidity. The air is always wet, and when it gets cold that wet air forcefully amplifies the chill. It seems to infiltrate everywhere, like an icy hand slid down the neck of a sweater.

This cold weather is inconsistent, though. It will be near freezing and miserably cold for a few days in December. But then a morning will arrive mild and pleasant, and people will wear shorts and eat their meals outside in courtyards rimmed by green tropical plants.

This uneven rhythm was maddening after Katrina without the benefit of electricity or gas. One day would be sunny and beautiful— the perfect time to let the sunlight and breeze freshen our battened-down houses, decent days to work on house repairs, to ride a bike to the French Quarter, and to sleep with the windows open. But the following day the weather could turn to debilitating cold. The old houses, so efficient at diffusing summer heat, seemed to collect and emanate the cold when it arrived. Walls and doors were cold to the touch, and so were faucets and cans of food. I gathered all the blankets and sheets I had, but it was never enough, so on the worst nights I simply slept in my clothes and my coat, scarf, and wool hat.

I tried to accept the cold as a necessary companion. I held out hope that it would kill the mold we were told was likely seething beneath our noses in every flood-touched cranny of our intricate, old homes. I came to think that the cold was an unpleasant but helpful part of our city's recovery—like riding in a car with someone who stinks badly of old garlic and fresh onions but who is also buying the gas for the trip.

But I also often thought of Ted on the very cold days, especially when I was psyching myself up for a quick shower. Ted was one of my neighbors before the storm. He was about my age, and he rented an apartment in a house that was just like mine. We were friendly when we saw each other and invited each other over whenever either of us had house parties. I saw Ted after the storm in early November hauling ruined furniture from his apartment, fully decked out in a breathing mask and rubber gloves. He asked me where I was living and I told him I was already back in my house and staying for good.

"Are you crazy? What are you going to do?" he said, almost shouting at me. "You know there won't be any utilities here for months, don't you? You're going to take cold showers in the winter? When it's thirty degrees? You're going to do that?"

When I thought of Ted on cold mornings, I also remembered how I wanted to punch him in the mouth that day. I knew he meant what he said without malice, that he just didn't believe anyone would want to put up with such conditions if they had other options. Maybe he was even legitimately concerned for my well-being. But at the time of that encounter it was still warm, and what I saw was a nervous little shit plugging me with questions about the future that I didn't want to ask myself. Long-term planning at the time meant one week to another, not a change in seasons. And there was Ted shooting holes in the confidence I had built up in the plausibility of simply moving back into my house and making do.

"Then don't fucking move back, Ted," I yelled hotly. I meant merely to say it, but it came out of my mouth as shouting. "I'm staying, do whatever the hell you want."

This uncomfortable exchange came to mind almost every time I stood in front of my shower, naked, with my bare feet balled up on the cold tile floor and the water running and running. Letting the water run was partly force of habit and also procrastination before an unpleasant task. I knew the water would not magically warm up no matter how long I kept it running. There was no forgetting, after all, that I had used a hacksaw to cut the flood-ruined hot water heater from its pipes and then rolled the thing violently down the alley and out to the curb, where it sat dented and stained for several weeks before a tractor carted it off. Anyway, there was no gas service in the neighborhood either.

So I was well aware of the obstacles standing between my naked body shivering in front of the tub and the prospect of taking a hot shower again in my own bathroom. But I stood there anyway, looking at the water, talking to the dogs, adjusting the wick on the lantern sitting on the bathroom's broken window frame. I was gathering courage, and weighing the relative merits of remaining rank and stale or turning my flesh to a blue tone under the cold water.

"Fuck you, Ted," I would say aloud before climbing into the shower. And it was a climb, starting first with one leg unfurled under the stream of water and then an arm and finally my chest thrust at the cold torrent. Those songs that kept me company while walking through the neighborhood on lonely nights served me well in the shower too, and I sang them at the top of my lungs while alternately cursing Ted, my new whipping boy and voodoo doll for the freezing winter shower.

I hatched a number of coping rituals to get on with my day-to-day life, and one of them amounted to frosting over a heart of winter. I decreed that self-pity would remain displaced for the duration of the crisis, like the storm evacuees still living in Atlanta or Houston, and to keep it at bay I adopted a stern and tough-minded interior voice. This seemed important. My own voice was practically the only one I would hear in my unhappy hermitage, I reasoned, so I might as well make sure it was a disciplined and positive voice, one that argued for the future and for the good times to come instead of wallowing in the present woes and worries. I was determined to screw a hard attitude down on my mind like the lid over a mason jar of bleeding-heart beets. Things would be tough and so would I.

At the end of a normal day I walked up to bed in the cold house, pushed off my shoes, turned up the collar on my coat, and pulled the wool hat down over my ears. In the candlelight I would find the dogs peering at me from the edge of the bed, looking doubtful and cold themselves. Sometimes I let them climb up and sleep around me on the mattress for warmth, replicating what I hear some Alaskan sled drivers would call a two-dog night. When everyone settled down, I would summon my inner drill sergeant and address the ceiling in a loud and dramatic voice, like a prosecutor facing a jury.

"What I am?" I would typically announce. "Am I a girl who needs her soft, lacey things to whisk her off to sleep? No. I'm happy to sleep in my coat and boots! Adventures are stirring in my dreams. I might as well be dressed to greet them!"

Even at the time I knew it was a bit overwrought, but the little pep talks still did wonders for my spirits. Books helped too. I had to forego reading in bed when I first moved back home, because I couldn't seem to gather enough candles close enough to the bed to see the pages. That changed when a friend lent me a sporty little headband that had a battery-powered lamp attached to it. I think he had it for bicycling at night, but it would be equally at home on a miner's helmet. In my house, it constituted the light of reason. I would strap the thing to my head, climb into bed, and have a direct beam of civilizing illumination at the command of my neck. Thus equipped, I flew through books. To fuel the courage of that drill sergeant in my head, I read Zorba the Greek and imagined the battle-scarred Alexis scoffing at my little discomforts. To carry myself away, I reread The Great Gatsby for the sixth time. I took on a history of World War I and felt decadent lying in my dry bed instead of a wet trench with shells falling. I read stories about the Dublin slums and thought about my long-gone relatives stepping seasick and penniless off Atlantic steamers in a world so much more alien to them than even flooded New Orleans was to me. Perspective was my secret weapon, and books gave me plenty of ammunition.

My perspective on a few specific things darkened for the worse, though, especially when it came to bumps in the night. I was always annoyed by hearing the movements and voices of other people through a shared wall, primarily because it cut through the illusion of privacy. Surely, anyone I could hear through the wall could hear me and whatever I might be doing as well. But lying in my bed on those winter nights, with the dark and silence pressing over me like taunting bullies, I realized I actually missed the occasional sounds of my own neighbors emanating through the wall from the apartment next door. I wished for even that little sign of life. Stomping feet, a name hollered down the stairwell, a dog barking at traffic, a door slamming shut—it all indicated life and activity, and I wanted it back.

But now there was nothing, and that's just how it sounded. There wasn't even the creaking, cricking commotion of nighttime nature you might hear outside the tent on a good, secluded camping trip. The silence was so complete, in fact, that when a noise did come along it was utterly nerve-wracking.

The houses and trees in the neighborhood were shredded. So when a bad windstorm blew through, the night came alive with tremendous, violent noise. I lay in bed on one such night trying to discern what was making each individual sound in the outdoor cacophony. Loose tarps were flapping with plastic roars on the neighbors' damaged rooftops like broken spinnakers in a gale. Aluminum siding, torn partially free, was slapping against houses, the impact sounding like new windows being smashed. Dangling tree branches scraped on walls and windows like fingers dragged on a chalkboard.

Sometimes the noise was much more specific and isolated, and that changed it from worrisome to terrifying. My longing for the sounds of my neighbors moving and living on the other side of my wall was largely nostalgic. For practical purposes, I did not want to hear sounds coming from the rooms next door at night when I knew the tenants were still way up across the state in Shreveport. So when I heard something like a single, careful footstep on the floorboards next door while I was in bed one night, neighborly affection was not my first emotion. Instead, I lay with my eyes wide open and tried to discern just what could have caused the sound.

The dogs seemed unconcerned, but I knew I had heard it and I couldn't stop picturing scenarios in my head. The house was completely dark. Maybe one of the street scavengers figured it was unoccupied and was getting ballsy. Maybe he came in through one of the missing windows over there, or maybe he had some little tool to defeat the deadbolt. It would be easy enough to break in once he assumed no one would be watching out in the deserted street or from any of the empty houses all around. The sound I heard might have been his footfall on the stairs as he crept to the bedrooms looking for loot that had escaped flood damage on the second floor.

I couldn't take it. I pulled myself out of bed quietly and stood up listening for the next sound, thinking about my next move. Call the police? But all I heard was a little noise in the night. Maybe I was overreacting. I could just yell something. But then what? If I yell and hear no response, then I haven't done myself any good. If I yell and hear someone tearing off downstairs, he might be headed over here or he might just hide and come back later. If he got in once, he could get in again.

So I didn't yell, and I didn't call the police. I brought the shotgun out from underneath the bed and grabbed a flashlight. I walked downstairs as silently as I could manage. But by moving around I had given the dogs hope for a midnight walk, so they started scampering around and making more noise on the wood floors than I ever could. I went outside with the gun and the light and unlocked the door to the apartment. It was just as dark as my side of the house, of course, and I pointed the light down the first few rooms. Being a novice at all this, it was only at this point—framed in the doorway and pointing a light into the dark—that I realized my hands were too full to actually use this fearsome shotgun very quickly if I needed to. I juggled my gear around a bit, but it didn't seem to make much difference. The shotgun required two hands to operate, and I needed to hold a light too.

Regardless, I walked inside and progressed to the base of the stairs. The house was completely quiet. Not even my dogs were making noise anymore. I shined the light up the stairwell. I didn't know what I was doing or why. This was, after all, my first attempt at an armed sweep of the house. I blundered my way upstairs, my hands still full with the gun and the light. There was nothing to find. I went in both the dark bedrooms and the bathroom and found nothing but the quick shadows of my light moving across the walls.

It had been a false alarm, but it had shaken me up nonetheless. I went back to my bedroom, stowed the gun again, and slipped into bed in my clothes. I stayed awake most of the night listening for noise with ears full of nothing.

When things were bad and fearful like this, I was glad to be on my own. I had no one else to answer to and no one else to consider with my sometimes erratic decisions. I could simply concentrate on getting myself through this bad time with my fictional drill sergeant and my goofy street songs. It was cold and desolate and unnerving. I knew it and I didn't want anyone else around to commiserate with. I didn't even want to know my friends, the ones who were in the city and working through their own difficulties in their own neighborhoods. I thought about Ted, that ex-neighbor, and his skeptical response when I told him I planned to stay in the house without lights or heat. I knew I never wanted to see him again.

The dogs sometimes looked up at me by candlelight, telling me with their intelligent eyes that they knew things were wrong. Sometimes they would freak out with special fury when I came home late on cold nights, flipping around like whirling dervishes in frantic displays of excitement and annoyance that I had kept them waiting so long curled up in the dark house. But they were easily placated with a walk and a biscuit. Dealing with another person—a child or a lover or even a roommate—would have made my situation much more complex. About all I could manage was to hunker down and let the time pass like the cold weather.

But on the warmer nights the house could be beautiful in its silence and candlelight glow. That's when I wished I wasn't alone, when I longed for a companion. I wanted someone to see this and experience this with me. I wanted someone to turn to and live it with, someone to be with.

I couldn't picture who this might be, but when I lay there on a good night—with an open window allowing a light breeze into the room and the big candles flickering their caramel light into the dresser mirror—I knew she would feel just as I did. Like me, she would be overwhelmed, fatigued, and needy. So it was easy to imagine how I would be with her. She would lie next to me and I would tell her what I was going to do, explaining that I would kiss her to sleep one part at a time. I'd tell her I would kiss her legs, and send them to rest after their long day hiking up broken escalators and standing in lines. I'd tell her I would kiss her belly, and shut it down now that it had done its best with the night's unsatisfying meal of canned food. I'd kiss her arms, weary from all the lifting and scraping and prying they'd done on the house repairs. I'd address special kisses to her hands and fingers, for their work filling in forms for insurance and disaster relief, for the grip they held on the phone while trying to find a human with answers in the distant corporate bureaucracies. I'd kiss her neck for keeping her head up as the world tried to bow it. I'd kiss her between her breasts, close to her heart as it descended into a restful pace with her sleep. I'd kiss her forehead and wish for peaceful dreams in her sleeping brain. I'd kiss her lidded eyes for all the beautiful and horrible things she'd seen in the day in our stricken New Orleans, and I'd kiss her ears, each one, to seal them up so that my lips would linger as the last sound she heard in the heavy silence of the night.

It was a pretty scene to conjure in the candlelight, though the dogs usually provided some reminder of their more corporeal presence in the room, sometimes groaning in their sleep, sometimes farting. Dr. Watson usually took a place at the threshold of the bedroom door like a snoring sentinel, while Ginger would belly-crawl under the bed to curl up next to the shotgun I had stashed in her favorite hiding spot. As long as she didn't climb up and pee on my quilts, I couldn't begrudge Ginger her old hiding spot under there. We all needed our own way of getting through the night.

Ten   The Katrina Christmas

It snowed in New Orleans on Christmas Day 2004, the Christmas before Katrina. It was a faint dusting, with fluffy wisps of the stuff coming down from a gray morning sky, and it melted as soon as it touched the warmer pavement. But it was the first time New Orleans had seen snow in many years, and the first time this freak precipitation had visited on Christmas Day in half a century.

No one was prepared for it. Highways closed down, stranding people on one side or the other of the Mississippi River and radically changing holiday travel plans. Mostly, though, people frolicked in the snowfall in the streets. They scooped up the little bits of snow that accumulated on car hoods to form snowballs, perhaps for the first time in their lives, or took pictures of their kids romping through the stuff in backyards hemmed in by palm trees that suddenly looked as misplaced in the snow as a giraffe stuck in the nativity manger.

I spent the day at a friend's house in the Treme, the beautiful, historic but drug-scarred neighborhood just north of the French Quarter. We did the snowball bit ourselves. We ran up and down a block that on a normal day we would traverse only with caution and an eye out for thugs. At the corner of the block, a barroom door opened and out walked Kermit Ruffins, a trumpet player and an endlessly gregarious New Orleans character who channels the spirit of Louis Armstrong in his jazz shows and everyday demeanor. He stepped outside wearing a Santa Claus hat and carrying a Budweiser longneck in one hand and his shining trumpet in the other. He stood on the corner for a minute with his fiancée. As the snow sailed down, blurring over the evidence of neglect on the ancient-looking Creole cottages around us, Kermit put his lips to his trumpet and blew a few bars of "Silent Night" before breaking into his well-known, benevolent laugh and taking a pull from his beer.

It was one of those rare and wonderful moments that, even as it was happening, I knew would have a special place in my memory forever. I even thought that this strange, snowy Christmas morning in the subtropics was fated to be the most magical holiday I would possibly experience in New Orleans. But, of course, I wasn't counting on Katrina and its power to drive a fissure through time, to create such a dramatic sense of prestorm life and poststorm life that it was sometimes hard to relate experiences on one side of that decisive line to life on the other.

My family asked me to come home to Rhode Island for Christmas. It was a tempting prospect, particularly as a field trip back to a fully functioning community filled with old friends and loving family members. But the more I thought about going back home, the more I realized I already was home. I knew the first holiday season after Katrina had to be something different. I wanted to be a part of making it special, something golden despite the tattered and gray shroud still hung over the desperate town.

I've always regarded Christmas as the Crescent City's secret holiday. Mardi Gras and Jazz Fest and Halloween and New Year's Eve are the famous party holidays, the marquee draws that make people hop in their cars or book flights to get down here and join the fray. But Christmas is stealth. Hardly anyone travels to New Orleans at Christmastime unless they are natives coming back to visit family. Invariably, the city turns on the charm for them, as if the whole place is collectively trying to lure its itinerant children back home.

What could anyone say when presented with the New Orleans holiday spread, a Creole cornucopia that might, depending on individual family traditions, include a dark, smoky gumbo, ropes of andouille, shrimp remoulade, redfish courtbouillon, deep-fried turkey injected with seasoning, oyster stuffing with almost as much oyster as stuffing, and pecan pie dense and sticky enough to challenge the most confident dentures? There is little else to say besides something like "damn, it's good to be home," muttered between bites and sips of potent sazerac cocktails.

Everywhere, the city's beautiful landscape of architecture is transformed for the season. New Orleans people throw themselves into the business of Christmas light displays and other home holiday décor with the same energy they devote to Halloween and Mardi

Gras costumes—and, as with those costumes, individual approaches can hew toward the classic and elegant or become riotous extravaganzas. The large Victorian houses Uptown can look like glittering sculptures of light on the holiday evenings, and some people even decorate their huge live oak trees so that the light displays sometimes continue right out over the street along the rambling, curving limbs. In less wealthy neighborhoods, the narrow, tightly spaced shotgun houses can be so enthusiastically decked with lights from one address to the next that the net effect looks like one contiguous display stretching on for practically the entire block without a discernable break. In the French Quarter, wrought iron balconies are traced out in strings of lights, and carriageway entrances are framed in green flocking. Some of the gas lanterns on the street even wear red Christmas bows as their orange flames warmly flicker away behind the beveled glass. The sentimentality of Christmases past—even the imagined ones from literature—always seem very much alive in the streets of New Orleans.

Somehow, Katrina made an unexpectedly redeeming contribution to all this, like a grinch who creeps in to steal presents but accidentally drops a wad of traveler's checks in his tracks. The mere appearance of Christmas lights in the parts of town that had electricity became that much more stirring for those of us living in the blacked-out neighborhoods, evoking new and humble wonder at simple beauty. Sometimes I would take Dr. Watson and Ginger out for a nighttime drive around Uptown. The dogs would stick their heads out the car windows, thrilled with the feel of wind blowing back their ear leather, while I had something like the same response gazing over the beautiful concentrations of golden and colored lights on the porches and iron fences and trees and balconies as we cruised along, with WWOZ playing sentimental old New Orleans songs and nary a functioning traffic signal to interrupt our slow, gliding tour.

On the way back home, as we drove deeper into the flood-ravaged neighborhoods leading to Mid-City, the gloom of the dark, blasted-out blocks was here and there broken by the odd FEMA trailer sitting on someone's yard and sporting a string of Christmas lights tacked up around the door. I always interpreted the little displays as equal parts holiday spirit, stubborn humor, and symbolic defiance on the part of the occupants of these lonely, otherwise stark and utilitarian emergency outposts. The little runs of Christmas lights were often the only twinkles of life for blocks around.

While the season's alternating dance of freezing to balmy days would continue all winter, by the middle of December I felt the first trickles of my own personal thaw running across my heart, that emotional core I had purposely frosted over for safekeeping earlier on. Everything remained the same at my house, and the neighborhood looked no different, but I could feel my mind and my emotions shifting gears as the days progressed toward Christmas. It was as though I was responding to some instinct, triggered by seasonal cues in all the now-distorted but still-familiar Christmas rituals. I wanted to come back to the fire, shoulder my way in among friends, and warm up again.

When I finally did begin to shake off that antisocial malaise I had cultivated in the dark, I wasn't a bit surprised to find my gregarious friend Keith Hurtt dangling a plan for merriment before my newly reopened eyes. He offered an invitation to a pre-Christmas outing that, on later reflection, seemed like something Charles Dickens and Tennessee Williams might have collaborated on if the two had somehow gotten drunk together at a tavern in the afterlife and conspired a twisted holiday production.

Keith called it the Santa Rampage, and he had been its de facto ringleader for years. We were to dress as Santa—or Mrs. Claus, or an elf, or whatever—and gather at a French Quarter bar early on the Sunday before Christmas Day, which is normally a bustling shopping day downtown. Our itinerary was simply to roam from bar to bar in costume, spreading cheer and gentle mischief before arriving at the community Christmas caroling event held in Jackson Square just after sundown.

"Join us!" Keith roared gleefully. "We go bar hopping, elbowing shoppers off the sidewalk and scaring the little kiddies!"

Keith prepares for his role in the Santa Rampage each year by taking a sack of charcoal briquettes into his backyard and chipping them down to little flints. He wraps each of these in red or green tissue paper and ties the little bundle with wrapping ribbon. Then he collects a harvest of twigs from a juniper bush near his fence.

These are his switches, and he dispenses them along with his freshly wrapped lumps of coal all day to unsuspecting passersby, innocent bar patrons, and delighted barmaids.

"And this is all you'll get!" he might advise them.

Or: "Remember, good girls get presents on Christmas but bad girls have more fun the other 364 days of the year. Take your coal now, it's worth the trade."

We met that Sunday afternoon at Molly's at the Market, the same Decatur Street bar that had stayed open through the raising of holy hell in early September.

"Santa, you're early," grumbled a guy in the corner.

"I'm not Santa, little boy," one of the Santas replied, sounding in practiced character. "I'm here as his emissary, and I'm here with a warning for all of you. Santa has great things in store for you on Christmas Day. But no one here has yet been good enough to deserve them! He'll have to put the stuff on ice unless you all can tip the scales. So, we need to see more niceness. Now, who wants to be nice and buy Santa's emissary here a Jameson's?"

A clutch of little shot glasses appeared before us in an instant and with a toast we were off for the day. There were only about a dozen variously costumed characters to our group, though we made enough noise for twice as many people as we wove our way down the sidewalk, ringing brass bells, blowing kazoos, and randomly shouting our group cry of "Ho! Ho! Ho!"

Shoppers and the odd National Guard patrol laughed and waved and honked from their passing cars, and after a few blocks we came upon Tujague's, an antique of a Creole restaurant in business since 1856. Here we planted ourselves at the long smooth bar and lit into the surprised patrons, a group of World War II–generation couples in Christmas sweaters who looked like they had come downtown for a festive day in the Quarter. Keith dispensed his presents

"There it is, kiddies, here's your coal," he said, placing a small, green-wrapped lump in each of their upturned palms. "And here's your switch."

"That's right, you bad, naughty boys and girls," I joined in, thrilled at the theater of it. "Now, onward to niceness, let this be a warning to you."

Everyone laughed, and one of the couples bought us drinks for another big, bar-wide toast. Outside, a group of children who had spotted us ducking into the bar were gathered around the door, some of them hiding themselves around the iron column in front and the boldest standing right there framed by the doorway, peering in at this disconcerting scene of adults acting strangely.

Back outside, we walked a few more merry blocks swigging from plastic cups of beer and mixed drinks all the way. We crossed Bourbon Street, and it was dead quiet with nearly as many bouncers and barkers hanging around the doorways as customers actually patronizing the big clubs. We turned down a side street and headed for the Erin Rose, a small pub where our visit was evidently anticipated.

"It's the drunken Santas!" yelled the bartender, who threw her hands in the air and startled the half-dozen barflies who had been quietly getting hammered prior to our arrival.

We trooped in from the street, an explosion of fur-lined red coats and red faces. We sparked up the jukebox in the corner, and in a moment the room was rolling. A girl in the corner wanted to dance. She sat at the bar in a red, bare-shouldered dress with a Japanese motif of dragons and lanterns in black stitching. Her hair was short and spiky and her chin dimpled with a shiny metal piercing. A much older man was sitting next to her, rubbing her forearm covetously as she rested it on the bar. But she ignored him and rose from her seat, grabbed one of the Santas, and demanded a dance in the tight space between the bar and the front windows.

"Dance with me, Santa!" she exclaimed to him turbulently, falling into a cackle of laughter as he complied. When the song ended she went back to her corner, though all the motion had left her somewhat disheveled. From across the room I saw a breast fall out of her strapless dress, which she recovered an instant later with a deft scoop of her hand to return it to safe cover. She sat there through the next song, but then got back on her heels when a more exciting swing number came on. She grabbed another Santa, who broke off whatever story he was telling us to dance with her.

But then Keith started clanging his bell, our signal for departure, and we were all moving back outside, bound for the next stop. Two people were hustling past at just the moment our jovial group burst onto the street. They were quick-walking their way to join the caroling. Our brains were smoky and soaked with beer, and we hollered at them and threw arms around them—strangers to the whole group—and they eagerly fell in under our dubious wings and accompanied us down to Jackson Square. The square was packed with people when we arrived, and all the families, couples, old people, and teenagers in the crowd were dressed warmly against the cold night. Most people clutched little candles rigged up inside paper cups to protect the flame from the breeze. It looked like a nighttime garden of soft lights. Above, the scene continued with the white Christmas lights strung along the iron balconies of the stately Pontalba apartments flanking the square. From a stage at the center of the square, choir members led the thousands gathered around them in Christmas songs. Everywhere, people stood grouped in circles as they read the familiar lyrics by the flickering candlelight.

Some of the Santas were making up their own words, adding a bawdy note when the impulse struck, but I resisted the urge and somehow managed to keep my mouth shut. It was enough to listen to the French Quarter singing again.

My office was quiet the day of Christmas Eve. The hours slipped by quickly and soon the day was over. I mounted my bicycle, but instead of trucking straight up Canal Street as usual I decided to take a circuit of the French Quarter. The old steamboat Natchez was tied up along the river nearby, and happy melodies were piping up from its boiling calliope to drift along the neighborhood's narrow streets. Large groups of people were clustered around Bourbon Street bars for Christmas Eve parties that had started at lunchtime, but otherwise there were only a few scattered couples and families or off-duty waiters walking the streets in their aprons.

I rode through Jackson Square under St. Louis Cathedral and the old Spanish government buildings to the quiet side of the Quarter where there are still more homes than hotels and restaurants. The sidewalks here were lined with piles of cut wood, the remains of storm-damaged trees from the cloistered rear courtyards. They were stacked neatly and sometimes tied together in bundles in the way that people who care about the French Quarter are compelled to arrange their trash, and with the backdrop of the old buildings they looked less like storm casualties and more like cords of firewood dropped off house by house by some nineteenth-century peddler. I looked up to the Christmas lights curled like ivy around the wrought iron balconies, and, as the gray winter sun dissolved into monotone over the other side of the building peaks, I imagined wood fires warming the drafty old Creole living rooms from yuletide hearths upstairs.

The music of the calliope faded the farther I rode through the Quarter. While some homes glowed, many other windows were dark, and streets were empty for blocks at a time. Shopkeepers closed early and the few street corner fortune-tellers who had made it back to town already had packed up their tables for the night and were wheeling them home in little carts at sunset. As I rode my bicycle through these quiet, half-darkened streets with the old-fashioned gas lanterns burning away on the brick walls, the sense of timelessness was overpowering. The modern glow and buzz was diminished, and somehow the silence sounded like Christmas to me.

Later that night, after a Christmas Eve dinner with friends, I took the Amazing Dr. Watson and Ginger on a long walk through the neighborhood. As the dogs sniffed the ground and the piles of noxious trash, I peered up at the façades of houses as part of my daily inspection of the stagnant neighborhood. After a few blocks, though, I spotted something new. I looked up from the street to a small house and could see a flicker through the little windows at the top of its front door. It looked like a candle's small, inconstant light, and it danced over the needles of a pine wreath nailed to the door. Surrounded by darkness and with the stars so visible above in the cold night, I slipped into the fantasy that I was walking through another century. I conjured more amber-hued Dickensian visions, hanging them on the humble glitter of that one weak candle and the gesture of a wreath. I pictured turkeys dressed and ready for the oven behind that door and a decorated Christmas tree ringed with brightly wrapped gifts for sleeping children and tobacco pipes and brown liquor set at the ready on the sideboard for the next day's feast.

The editor of reason in my head reminded me that whoever had hung that wreath was probably sitting inside near that candle, just as cold in the house as I was in the street. He might be wondering if he had heard footsteps outside or the jingle of a dog leash, and he might be fetching his gun. He might be watching me through a blacked-out window.

But back in my happy visions, the Christmas scene was cooking as warmly as the imagined goose in the oven, and the details of the life under that roof were as rich as the fat bubbling under the skin of the roasting bird. In my head, it was Victorian London, and Scrooge in his bedchamber dreamed of his old school, and Cratchit's children dreamed of dinner and sturdy crutches for Tiny Tim.

The dogs and I walked on through the shadowy wilds of the neighborhood. We ended up by the cemeteries, home to acres of raised tombs and angel statues that had stood fast with their wings and up-stretched arms as everything flooded around them after Katrina. I noticed the sound of bells tolling out a Christmas carol through the dark. It was no Santa-themed ditty, but a real churchy song, "The First Noel." I could hear the words in my head, and they joined the scraps of the Dickensian fantasy glowing in there. "Born is the king of Israel, Born is the king of Israel."

I aimed the dogs toward the sound and we walked through streets that seemed filled with nothing but the tone of the bells. After a few blocks we turned a corner and were in front of the whitewashed edifice of St. Anthony of Padua Church as the music continued to emanate through the cold air from its steeple several stories above.

I stood there for a while with the dogs. Ginger dithered about nervously, her ears trying to orient the disembodied sound around her. Otherwise, all was still. Most likely, the music was a recording and someone had pushed a button hours ago to set it playing. It must have been connected to a battery or generator inside. There was no sign of anyone around, no cars except the destroyed and stripped ones parked at crazy angles to the curb. I looked up Canal Street at the cemetery and back down the other way and saw nothing moving in the darkness between the church and downtown's skyline of blacked-out skyscrapers in silhouette.

Certainly, anyone else who might have been staying in the houses around here on this Christmas Eve would be hearing this music as they shivered together in their dark rooms. Without TVs or stereos or any other noise, it would fill their homes much as it did the streets. I wanted to be in one of those rooms now, holding some imaginary companion, hearing the bell music in the night through the thin walls, hearing it ride on the moonlight that would hit us as it came in through the plastic tarps stapled over the missing windows.

I stood in the middle of Canal Street. I imagined myself through the eyes of someone up there where the bells were ringing in the steeple. From that perch, he could survey all the surrounding houses with their threadbare roofs and crumbled chimneys and the walls that had been sheared off to show the dollhouse view of bedrooms inside. He could see the decimated treetops and the empty fields and the gray stripes of road going like straight, parallel canals toward the river, silent and empty. He could look down and see me standing there looking back up at him with my overgrown hair peeking out from my wool cap and my shoulders hunched in my pea coat. He would see my two dogs—the big yellow one standing there bored and immobile, the other ratty one twitching and groaning with nervous impatience. In the old world scene in my head, there was an abbot up there in the steeple, solemn in his bell duties and enlivened on a tipple, pulling the belfry rope but also pulling on a flask of something strong he brought up against the weather. And I was the night watchman with my hounds, patrolling the blocks on the silent night before Christmas. All is well. It's quiet and cold and that's perfectly all right for this yesterday village conjured in my mind. All is well. "Born is the king of Israel," the bells were singing in my head.

I walked back to my block about a mile away, where the shattered cars lay in the moonlight and the only movement was the flame on the candle I had left lit on the porch during my walk as a friendly beacon for others who might be out. And then I was back inside the house to fumble for the lighter and lamps, to toss the dogs their treats, to look around at the nothing-to-do, nowhere-to-sit situation in the first-floor rooms and then climb upstairs to bed. It was too cold to do anything else but tuck in for another night sleeping in the coat and hat, under the blankets with a lamp left burning on the nightstand for heat. I closed my eyes to envision the wine I would drink with friends the next day on Christmas morning.

Eleven   Mardi Gras

Before New Orleans, the holiday seasons of my life always seemed to move at the same, normal pace. From Thanksgiving through New Year's, there were enough parties and visits to relatives and buffets and such that the rest of the slow, cold New England winter arrived like a welcome respite by the end of it. My first year in New Orleans, however, made clear that all of that would from now on be merely a prelude to the main event—Carnival.

There is less than a week between New Year's Day and the next major holiday on the city's peculiar local calendar, Twelfth Night, so named because it falls twelve days after Christmas on January 6. Its origins go far back into Christian history, and the story can be traced further to pre-Christian roots, but before I moved to New Orleans I only knew of it as the title of a gender-bending Shakespeare play.

But here, just about everyone knows that Twelfth Night means the start of Carnival season. Beginning promptly at midnight, a few moments into the morning of January 6, the DJ on duty at WWOZ's packed little radio studio will triumphantly start spinning Mardi Gras songs from a canon of street-beat anthems inevitably led off by the blaring sax heralds of "Carnival Time." Some people throw house parties, no matter if Twelfth Night falls on a Saturday or a Wednesday, and kids at school are reminded of why the day is important and share round, glazed, Mardi Gras king cakes in the classroom. That evening, a semisecret group of masked revelers commandeers a streetcar and with their brass band playing at the tail end proceed on a ceremonial ride downtown, dancing in the lurching, halting car, slinging beads to people on the sidewalk, and hoarsely heralding the start of Carnival season. Over the weeks that follow, the momentum builds in tempo, very slowly at first, then frantically in its last few days, until the whole thing reaches its great crescendo on Mardi Gras day, Fat Tuesday, the most celebrated day in a city of celebrations.

Soon after the dread year 2005 turned into 2006, we started hearing questions about whether Mardi Gras would happen. Friends from up north called wondering if it would be cancelled. Commentators all over the national media speculated on the chances for Mardi Gras, and their consensus prognosis fell somewhere between disbelief and disapproval. Some clearly just couldn't imagine New Orleans having Mardi Gras with so many of its people still displaced across the country and the city's own situation so precarious.

I chalked that up to a lack of imagination. For people living in the city that winter, there was no question of whether Mardi Gras would happen. Our mantra was "now more than ever," and if it had been put to some kind of official referendum it would have been a landslide in favor of floats and masks and beads. But nothing like a vote was needed. Mardi Gras is not held or hosted by the city of New Orleans, like a Fourth of July fireworks display is put on by a municipality or the Super Bowl is managed by the NFL. Mardi Gras issues forth from the homes and clubs and bars and streets of New Orleans, a product of the city's collective imagination and shared history. It is the central and defining cultural event of the city, and if it were made illegal by government decree, New Orleanians would still make it happen, like some bootleg, speakeasy Mardi Gras of revolutionary revelry.

So of course Mardi Gras was on for post-Katrina New Orleans, and that was the answer my hometown friends wanted to hear. They wanted to come down and see things for themselves and open their wallets for the stricken city. But their wallets were not fat, so they needed to crash at my place. They were bringing friends too, and by the time the last of their planes landed at Louis Armstrong New Orleans International Airport there would be six of us sharing the house with the two antsy dogs.

At least they were arriving after some massive improvements on the home front, including the return of lights and hot water. In January, the electrician who had been steadily working one ruined house to the next around the neighborhood discovered that I was living in my place and bumped me up to the top of his list ahead of others who were staying elsewhere. He rewired the old house in a startlingly short few days. My friend Charlie Blanque from around the corner showed me how to hook up and light the new gas-fired water heater in my moldy, disintegrating shed, and with that my utilities were back in business. Niceties like a phone line or Internet service would have to wait months more, but that hardly seemed important when I took the first hot shower in my house, laughing now at the cold breeze poking through the plastic tacked up over my missing windowpanes. It was beginning to feel much more like home. I paid the electrician with the very end of the money I had stashed, begged, and borrowed and just hoped my reluctant insurers would eventually come good on my policies.

While my Mardi Gras guests would have these basic household comforts, I warned them there would be little else. There was no money left for a refrigerator, and anyway the kitchen itself was still a gutted wreck. Eating at home still usually entailed cans of beans or stocking a cooler with ice each day. I put air mattresses in the living room with its ragged walls of exposed, bleach-splattered framing studs and dangling plaster shreds. I explained to them that the accommodations would be a little like earning squatters rights. In my once charming New Orleans neighborhood there were still few signs of people, no streetlights and no stores for ice, gas, toilet paper, food, or anything else within a mile or so. Cab dispatchers could make no assurances that a car would come out to the urban wilderness if we called one, and there was no public transit. Red Cross volunteers still drove through the rutted streets during the day calling people out with their bullhorns to get donated rations of macaroni, hand sanitizer, and bottled water. Every day, the debris-moving crews still chopped at the ramparts of former possessions and hauled them through the streets in dusty, broken loads.

Greater than my concern with the household logistics of hosting a half dozen people was my worry about how the city would seem to these visitors. I subjected them to a little pretravel counselling. I told them to expect a city full of upset people, a skeleton crew of a population racked with anxiety and stress but still determined to paint on a happy face for the sake of their town's favorite season. We were all feeling our way through this experience, I explained, and no one was confident about how it would end up.

We were giddy but jumpy, eager to celebrate our city and show the world we were back, but we deeply dreaded some spark, some crazy violence or even innocent mishap in the mayhem of Mardi Gras that could ruin it all and spin us down further still. We were unsure if the old clothes of celebration would fit after all the distortions our city had been through.

Even the people who most keenly anticipated Mardi Gras were wary of how it would all look from the outside. New Orleans culture in general is hardly ever conveyed to the rest of the world in anything like the way it feels to locals. Even under normal circumstances, Mardi Gras with all its decadent displays is a particularly easy target for clucking tongues. There is an alluring spectacle to debauched tourists acting out, flashing their fellow camera-laden tourists, trying to shock perverted cabbies and the nonplussed cops. But how to convince newcomers that, despite all that business, what really gets me excited is the thought of people my grandparents' age holed up in the back rooms of their Creole cottages methodically assembling costumes to wear out on the streets for Mardi Gras? It's hard to make a sound bite or video clip that communicates the encompassing fun of all the countless little unofficial parades that break out with their sardonic themes and beads recycled from years past and homemade musical instruments. There is magic in the spontaneous glee and bonhomie of one of these homemade processions rambling out of a side alley or down from a porch, its members instantly inviting you to join them. A moment later you might be swirling with the group in a riot of color and noise and sunshine on brass instruments and plastic beads flying and hand slaps and hand claps with smiling strangers. Joining in and offering up generous participation, doing your part to make the city ring with cacophonous, infectious joy, playing your role in the unscripted theater of the costumed street—that's what Mardi Gras means to the locals who embrace it.

Frat boys chanting from Bourbon Street corners and biker chicks thrilling the amateur videographers from hotel balconies are certainly part of Mardi Gras. Another is the visible wonder on the faces of children raised here who know that at Mardi Gras time the world of workaday adults and rules gives way to plastic-jeweled royalty. The same streets that bring them to school or the doctor's office are for a few days littered with toys and treasure tossed their way by benevolent strangers, masked by their costumes and deep in their cups.

Mardi Gras, at its best, can make you believe in New Orleans, in its magic and its fun and its romance. In that winter after Katrina, at the tail end of that dark and terrible season of night, New Orleans needed magic, fun, and romance. It needed believers and it needed Mardi Gras.

My guests were seasoned bartenders from Providence, Rhode Island, and they were coming to town not only to see Mardi Gras but to work it. The labor shortage for just about any type of job was acute, and they easily lined up temporary gigs slinging drinks at a tourist bar on Bourbon Street.

I wanted them to have some perspective on the disaster before they got to work. So directly after the airport pickup, our first order of business was a visit to the Lower Ninth Ward. There were plenty of other destroyed neighborhoods closer to home, like Lakeview, seat of the city's middle class, which had been nearly as badly ravaged. For that matter, the wreckage and gloom in my own little corner of the city was still sufficient to bring people to tears the first time they saw it. But for a one-stop education on the full fury of Katrina and the waste of its aftermath, there was nothing like a cruise through the Lower Ninth Ward.

This was an old neighborhood of modest and sometimes dilapidated homes bordered closely on two sides by industrial shipping channels. The levees on these channels burst with such force after the storm that the water blasted houses off their foundations and wrapped cars around telephone poles. We were nearly six months out from the disaster by this time, and the Lower Ninth Ward still looked as though the flood had washed through just the day before. Houses were sickeningly warped, their rooflines and even windows twisted in funhouse distortions. Big trucks still lay on their sides, upside down, or at whatever crazy angle they had been tossed by the torrent of exploding water. Kids' toys littered the streets amid tangles of every other sad, common household item. Recovery teams with cadaver dogs still periodically found human remains in the twisted wreckage. During our visit the only people around were a few young Common Ground volunteers bivouacked around the still-standing structures, hanging out under lean-tos made from blue tarps, smoking cigarettes, and giving the evil eye to sightseers like us.

The mood in the old, grumbling Cadillac was grim as we motored back across the Industrial Canal to the relatively unscathed Bywater. The visitors didn't know what to say, and I didn't feel like repeating any kind of commentary. Instead, I suggested we all go get a drink, and the heavy heads in the car nodded affirmative. I steered down a side street and told them we could visit Bud Rip's, a century-old neighborhood bar with a pressed tin ceiling, a barbershop in the back room, and a buzzer on the front door.

We were only a few blocks into the Bywater when a man pedaled a bicycle slowly into the intersection at Burgundy Street and came to a deliberate halt in front of our bumper. He wore a wig on his head and held a plastic cup of red wine. He was motioning for us to hold back, like a cop directing traffic, and right behind him came the procession. There were no floats, no police, and no spectators besides us in the car and some others looking out of the windows and front doors of their shotgun houses. But there was no mistaking that this was a parade.

About sixty people strutted and slow-rolled down the street while we idled at the intersection. I recalled seeing a flier for this somewhere downtown. The parade had started at a nearby wine store called Bacchanal and was named the Krewe de Screw—nominally, at least, in honor of the corkscrew. The casual cadence was set by a few guys with marching band instruments, a snare drum and a big bass drum in the lead, someone else on a tarnished saxophone, and then a few trombones. There was a guy shuffling along in a mermaid costume that hobbled his ankles, while women in can-can skirts and high heels pranced with exaggerated steps down the center of the street. There were huge, colorful headdresses everywhere. A man wearing a jolly pig mask pedaled from the rear of a tandem bicycle, while on its front seat, lashed to the handlebars as if steering, was a skeleton dressed in lingerie, looking like it had been liberated from a medical school.

As the Rhode Island guys and I watched the parade from the car, a strand of beads sailed through the open window and landed in my lap. I looked up from this surprise gift and saw Keith Hurtt grinning at me. He was decked out in a white tuxedo coat with tails and a top hat festooned with flowers.

"What are you doing in that boat? The flood's over!" he said.

"Where's the next stop?" I asked.

"Bud Rip's! Join us!" he called back, merging back into the body of the parade.

This was exactly the type of serendipity I needed to properly introduce the Rhode Islanders to the happy tides of Mardi Gras. We were headed to Bud Rip's anyway, where I expected we would stew for a time in the malaise of our visit to the Lower Ninth Ward. Instead, we drove a few more blocks and joined a parade party that had started out on the street, poured into the old bar, and would later continue down the street again. The men with the brass instruments and drums marched into the room and began playing as others lined the bar and called out for beers. Outside, a flatbed truck pulled up to the corner carrying a bunch of guys with electric guitars, amps, and drums, and they laid into a loud set of rock tunes. I had to look very closely at one bare-chested guitarist to see that he was wearing any clothes at all as he sat on the edge of the flatbed, rocking away in the gathering sunset.

Moments like this make Mardi Gras, these homegrown displays of goodwill and good times, these little traditions that often start with a dozen or so friends stringing together a plot in a barroom or around a kitchen table or out at a sidewalk party for one of the big-time parades.

In the guidebooks and the newspaper, top Mardi Gras billing goes to the magnificent, multimillion-dollar productions with celebrity grand marshals and society girls as their queens and businessmen and heirs as their officers. Sometimes you can buy your way into these groups. For others, scoring membership can entail a complex web of social standings, business contacts, and family connections. But joining the little ad hoc Mardi Gras processions and rolling parties can be as easy as going with the flow. Finding out about them is often just a matter of overhearing someone yakking about his own plans or maybe spotting a flier tacked to a coffee shop wall.

One of the better known of these productions was the Ninth Ward Marching Band, a group that found itself overemployed in this first poststorm Carnival season. For years, the band had taken to the street with an array of familiar marching band instruments and uniforms, plus cheerleaders, baton twirlers, and even a rifle corps. But the band is not affiliated with any school or sports team. Rather, it is roughly organized as a group of people, mostly in their thirties, who share an affinity for the Bywater, a wildly diverse neighborhood just over the Industrial Canal from the Lower Ninth Ward.

The fact that they could mount a full horn and drum line and march in time put the group in high demand from the traditional Mardi Gras krewes, which normally enlist high school marching bands to be part of their parades. The chance to play in a Mardi Gras parade is one reason the marching band tradition is such a popular extracurricular activity in New Orleans schools and helps explain why so many kids grow up here with the ability to wail on a trumpet, trombone, or tuba the way other kids can play video games or soccer. But in the winter after Katrina, very few high schools were open again in the area, and most of the instruments, uniforms, and gear were flooded. So the scarcity of bands was extreme, and into the void stepped the adult members of the Ninth Ward Marching Band.

None of the big Mardi Gras parades ever go through the Bywater, but the Ninth Ward Marching Band brought its show to the neighborhood for a miniparade all its own. I was taking some of the Rhode Islanders on a bike ride around town on the drizzling Saturday before Mardi Gras when we first caught sight of them. The red-fringed white uniforms of the high-stepping dancing girls out front announced their progress down a gray, chilly Chartres Street. At first, only a few people in caps and scarves had ventured outside to watch, but, as the music and banners and commotion pushed on down the street, more and more people followed up behind the parade, joining in by dancing and clapping and swelling the procession's numbers. By the time the band made it to Mimi's bar, the street was clogged with people and was effectively, if unofficially, shut down to traffic. The band played its brassy arrangements of "Rock You Like a Hurricane" and "House of the Rising Sun" before breaking up. Everyone congregated at the bar for a while, and eventually the band members set off in small groups, headed home or to the next party, done up in their red and white band uniforms and blowing single notes and bugle calls into the rainy streets as they walked.

In the final few days before the climax of Mardi Gras, groups like the Ninth Ward Marching Band were joined by a pageant of other parades and bands of friendly pranksters and casually organized revelers. They are so loose and fluid in nature that no one can really keep tabs on them all, but one of the largest must be the Society of St. Anne. Early on the morning of Mardi Gras day itself, the first of the St. Anne revelers emerge from the side streets of the Faubourg Marigny and Bywater neighborhoods sporting elaborate homemade costumes. The group grows as more people join, block after block, until it becomes a huge, freeform stream of costumed merriment winding through the streets of the French Quarter.

Compared to the escorted, regimented, and officially recognized parades rolling along St. Charles Avenue, these little groups are often chaotic and confusing. They can be hard to find, but if you do, their prime virtue of instant inclusiveness assures membership. Some of them have been going on for years, but, like a lot of grassroots activities, they still rely on the enthusiasm of a few people to show up and make them happen. After Katrina scattered so many of the city's most colorful feathers, it was a fair wager whether this or that favorite Mardi Gras event would materialize this year.

But all around town, these independent and sometimes overlapping groups of Mardi Gras celebrants did their thing, resuscitating the traditions that put their own personal stamp on the holiday. The weekend before Mardi Gras, a congregation of fanciful flying things formed up in Jackson Square for the enchanting little Krewe du Faye Fairy Parade. Dressed as ladybugs, birds, bees, and fairies with all manner of wire wings and colorful stockings and bustiers, they departed at nightfall for a meandering tour of the French Quarter. Somewhat more debonair but no less spirited was the revival of the Krewe of Cork, a group begun by local chefs, wine merchants, and sommeliers who dress themselves in wine-inspired costumes. Some four hundred of them assembled this year, dressed like Romans, like royalty, like walking champagne bottles, like the Blue Nun of German wine fame, like the much-derided box of wine.

Another group set out to test the notion that the difference between tuneful music and just plain noise is in the ear of the beholder. This self-proclaimed Crew of Joyful Noize got started around midnight as Lundi Gras turned into Mardi Gras with a cacophony of electric wailing. At point was Jessica, a bartender from Pal's Lounge, who was selected to be grand marshal for a procession with all the distorted formality of a postapocalyptic punk rock wedding march. She strutted in front of her chaotic flock in a transparent mesh top, checkerboard tights, vinyl hot pants, red go-go boots, and a police riot helmet. The band behind her featured not a single conventional instrument but rather a collection of noiseful inventions including a megaphone fused with a sax, a tuba made from plastic drainpipes, an accordion equipped with guitar pedals and air horns, drums fashioned from water coolers, and countless other variations. Megaphones and klaxons blared sirens, and the laser-like beams of handheld searchlights lanced over the brick walls and balconies of the Marigny streets as the group progressed toward the French Quarter.

Passersby fell in behind the group, often finding inspiration in the storm debris piled in the street for some simple new instrument to use along the way. A guy started banging a splintered two-by-four against a strip of sheet metal, and someone else used a warped bicycle wheel as an off-kilter xylophone, tapping the various spokes with a length of household plumbing.

A lone policeman intercepted the group at Esplanade Avenue, his glare steady but his arms waving wildly for attention. Jessica proved capable and quick in her grand marshal duties, though, and simply redirected the parade down the street. The whole group of forty or so people ducked into a Decatur Street bar before any further official intervention could be organized. The bar was already crowded as the parade filed in, and electronic house music was blaring from the dark dance floor in the rear. Band members continued their "noize" and, as though choreographed, immediately climbed up on the bar. They banged their water jug drums on the bar top and let the static chords fly, quickly overtaking the volume of the DJ's dance music. The bartender on duty was a neighborhood character named Joey who, as usual, was wearing a short, tight skirt around his slim hips, fishnet stockings over his hairy legs, and disco ball earrings on either side of his crew cut. He continued pouring drinks, handing them to customers around and through the legs of the costumed "noisicians" blaring away just above him.

One school of thought on Mardi Gras revelry is that the whole point is to get so full of wine and noise and fun and debauchery that you welcome the penance and deprivation that follows. Catholics, of course, call this period Lent, which starts the day after Mardi Gras, on Ash Wednesday. We were almost there, and the wear and tear in the packed Mid-City house was becoming acute. But it was more than the dizzying pace of parades and costume changes and late nights. There was an emotional toll that was new this year. It came from the discordance of all our smiling and laughter in an environment that could in an instant become overwhelmingly depressing and infuriating. If anyone suffered an injury that we couldn't tend at home, I knew we would have to take a trip to the city's bizarre emergency room, a facility that had been operating out of a flood-damaged Lord & Taylor department store since the storm. This was the extent of emergency medical services for a major American city—hospital beds and heart monitors set up where the shoe department or cosmetics counter used to be in an abandoned retailer— and still Mardi Gras was ringing through the streets.

Even those who could dodge the flood-battered neighborhoods could not escape the weight of the Katrina legacy that season. It even showed up in some float themes in the major parades. Some Carnival krewes traditionally take a biting, satirical view of New Orleans politics, and their members often toss beads from floats that are designed as elaborate jibes at local officials and their constant scandals. This year their cups of derision overflowed with material that hit everyone very close to home. There was a float depicting suburban police forces blockading the Mississippi River bridge to keep New Orleans residents from escaping their flooded city. While I was in Baton Rouge in the days after the storm, several of my friends had been turned back at gunpoint on that bridge and forced to wander back along the scorching highway and find some other means of survival. Another parade float showed the Superdome as a fiery gumbo pot in which helpless people were being boiled. Other floats attacked the media, FEMA, the U.S. Army Corps of Engineers, the mayor and the governor, and just about anyone else with an official role in the disaster.

The Krewe of Muses, an all-female organization that puts on one of the most popular parades, dedicated the last float of its procession to those lost to Hurricane Katrina and symbolized their absence by running the float with no riders. It rattled past the parade goers as a moving tribute, its decks empty, its bead racks bare. The cheers and bright yelling from the sidewalk and neutral ground ceased as it passed. There was only the grinding sound of the tractor pulling it and the crunch of its wheels on the beads littering the street. Ghostly white blossoms and shapes of flowing water decorated its flanks, and at its stern was a banner with script reading: "We celebrate life. We mourn the past. We shall never forget." The man operating the tractor was bent humbly, like a hearse driver. The bust of a Grecian figure at the prow of the float had a prominent papier-mâché tear beneath her eye. In the wake of this float, some onlookers had real ones filling their own.

On Lundi Gras—the day before Fat Tuesday—I told a friend that I was planning to set an alarm to get an early start on the next day's festivities.

"You have to set an alarm?" she asked with real astonishment. "God, I just spring right out of bed at dawn I'm so excited."

We were all excited, and a little surprised as well. Those arguments that maybe Mardi Gras shouldn't happen this year were unthinkable, but at the same time it was hard to see just how New Orleans could manage to pull it off. Somehow it happened, and there are plenty of people who will testify that it was the best Mardi Gras ever. There was no avoiding the omnipresent evidence that our city was pained and crippled, but we chose to decorate its crutches with colorful fringe and put face paint over its scars in the name of having and sharing a good time.

All day on Fat Tuesday, the huge, beaming smiles were everywhere. It seemed like the same expression no matter where we turned—on the faces of young people chasing parade floats, old people kicking back on the porch, and whole families out with their kids in matching costumes. Everyone was participating. Even the police—the beat cops overseeing the madness on the streets, the guys escorting the parades, the mounted officers clopping by on their horses—even they seemed happy. These were familiar rituals and roles, the stuff people grew up doing and seeing and dreaming about, and we hadn't missed a year despite all the unthinkable nightmare scenarios that had befallen us.

It also turned out to be a great year for the revival of costuming, which is one of the prime ways people participate in Carnival. Whether it's a simple little smock sewn by a mom the night before or an elaborate construction requiring assistants to enrobe, costumes are the means for anyone to add his or her own little blossom of mirth to the street, the stage on which the holiday is celebrated. And just like the float makers, everyday people had plenty of Katrina-related inspiration for new costume ideas. Satire and gallows humor ruled the day, and the streets were like fluid galleries of creativity. Purple, green, and gold may be the traditional colors of Mardi Gras, but this year the most common color for costumes was the bright, sunny-sky blue of plastic tarps, the roofing Band-Aid that had become practically the symbol of the storm's aftermath. It was fashioned into gowns and tuxedos, body wraps, elaborate headgear, and utilitarian, hardware store lingerie, all of it folded, taped, bent, and tied like the origami of dark humor.

There were the familiar Carnival-time problems as well—people who don't drink well, the hustlers and crooks, and the few distorted Christians who turn up each year to hurl biblical damnation on strangers. But even those bad elements were especially minor this year. Much of the joyfulness of Mardi Gras always comes from a feeling of fellowship when so many people turn out not just to watch but to participate, and that was in overwhelming display as everyone seemed to try extra hard to wring the maximum pleasure and goodness from the climax of the season.

The revelry was still pitted by sudden moments of intense sadness and gloom. It was the same weight again, surfacing as disbelief, heart-racing anxiety attacks, inexplicable tears streaking the carnival makeup and setting the painted lip aquiver for just a single minute before diving down and leaving a calm, stunned surface. They were feelings that proved hard to reconcile but were undeniable and, like the good times and fun, they too were something many of us shared together. In the open-hearted spirit of the day, friends would laugh and sing one moment, then turn their heads down and disclose these disconcerting emotions in the manner of a counseling session. And in a second they would be back on their feet to play with another group of familiar faces or fantastic costumes materializing out from the thick crowd of the street. Our hearts were exhausted, and, in the surge of feeling that Mardi Gras brought, people seemed to swing between glee and rage, hope and anguish.

But Carnival season was its own form of therapy. There had been an air of desperation at the beginning. If there was a group prayer, it might have been something like, "Please, God, let us just do this right and not be humiliated yet again in the eyes of the world. Let people see how unique and wonderful this place really is."

Yet once the celebration got rolling, the whole thing seemed like one big endorsement of the city, a living, sweaty, friendly, buzzed dissertation on the reasons why people still want to live here and fight through the difficulties.

While people continued to pack up and move away, others made Mardi Gras their deadline to return. The day is so huge in the mental calendar of residents and the annual pace of the city that people who have lived here can't escape its shadow even when they've moved elsewhere. Mardi Gras day is just another Tuesday everywhere else in America outside south Louisiana, and even under normal circumstances that stark reality has been known to drive New Orleans expatriates back to the city's arms. This year, six months after Katrina, the pull was in full effect. We bounced into people on the streets who were coming back after trying to live for half a year since the storm in other cities without the old magic.

For a day, at least, shattered New Orleans felt like the ultimate small town. In the thick press of people around the downtown parade routes and along the close, balcony-lined French Quarter streets, a happy reunion of friends and prestorm neighbors broke out at every turn. People were so happy to see each other they sometimes forgot their faces were heavily obscured by makeup or costumes. They saw old friends, threw their hands up, screamed their names, and charged toward them with incoming hugs before considering that the objects of their affection could not possibly recognize them beneath all the masks and feathers.

But it didn't seem to matter to the people rushing around with that kind of love on this kind of day. It was a time for New Orleans to share its hugs and tears, its drinks and its beads, its hope and fear, its big, big spirit and its defiance and most of all the joy of its grandest day. It was catharsis on a massive level.

"Honey," I overhead one woman tell another on the street, her voice rasping with emotion, "I'm so glad to be back home, I'm even happy to see people I hate."

Twelve A New Normal

The return of electricity and hot water at my house launched my own creature comforts into the stratosphere, but it did nothing for the frazzled nerves of Ginger. My troubled little foundling dog remained as anxious as ever. She still preferred hiding somewhere in the house, and failing that always had her back to a wall when in repose, scanning at all times for as-yet unseen threats. She seemed to jump out of her bristly, ratty fur at almost any loud or sudden noise, like a crash of thunder, the bap-bap-bap reports from the nail guns going off from roofs and scaffolding on reconstruction jobs all over the neighborhood, and sometimes even the rumble of a big dump truck hauling debris over a pothole in the street outside. When she got the chance, she still sometimes chewed up a valuable object or peed on something left on the floor.

She hit the Rhode Island crew a few times while they were around for Mardi Gras, peeing on one guy's pillow and chewing a fatal hole in another's air mattress. I explained to them that this too was part of earning their squatters rights for free Carnival lodging, and I thought they took it pretty well. By that point in my Ginger tenure, I had changed my sheets and bleached my mattress probably eight times after her urinary assaults, and I felt like a grizzled veteran lecturing fresh recruits about the hazards of the territory. But one day not long after Mardi Gras I got a bit too casual with the volatile little dog myself. I left my bedroom door open, and as surely as the tough-talking hero always takes shrapnel in the World War II movie, I returned at the end of the day to find that my freaked-out little dog had once again nailed my bed.

This spurred a trip to buy new bed sheets at the local Target in neighboring Metairie. Since the storm, I had made plenty of supply runs out of the suburbs, that other world where the modern housing and chain stores had largely been spared flooding because only one side of the pathetic federal drainage canal that forms part of the parish border had burst during the storm. As it happened, of course, the old city got the bad break on that deal. So a New Orleanian with a shopping list that ran deeper than the inventory of the average gas station required a trip to the suburbs, an experience that offered a fully functioning economy of boxy national chain stores but also promised the type of culture shock typically suffered by foreign exchange students.

On the short trip to the highway I drove past yet another beached boat, a pleasure cruiser all battered, stained with muck, and grounded on the sidewalk near a bus stop where no bus had stopped for more than six months. Then I merged onto the highway, joined the flow of fast-moving taillights, and later veered down an exit to be inserted into the middle of the gleaming suburbs. At night at least, with all the signs for fast food and oil changes and bank loans and gas prices and furniture lit in red against the uniformly beige suburban buildings, it looked as though nothing had happened to this part of the world. It was all the same inside the stores too. Down one aisle at Target, I spied a girl looking over the selection of picture frames while her boyfriend talked distractedly into a cell phone and held her earlier selections. A few yards away, a mother was trying to keep a swarm of children out of the colorful racks of ladies' underwear while maintaining the forward momentum of her laden shopping cart toward the bank of checkout lanes. Later, I drove back across the canal and the parish line into the dark. The difference between here and there felt so extreme I wished I had brought a camera. I could just about see myself putting together a slideshow to show friends the extent of my exotic travels one parish over.

Back home, I leashed up the dogs for a walk around the neighborhood. We turned up Palmyra Street, which looked curiously orderly simply because the piles of debris by the houses were newly formed and had yet to blow around. The night was lovely, with a faint breeze and temperatures in the high sixties. A block into our walk, Dr. Watson and Ginger both tensed up. A huge but friendly-looking dog was bounding up to us, followed a beat later by his owner hollering his name. This unknown dog went about sniffing Watson and Ginger until his owner could get a hold of him. All the while, a woman's voice called out the dog's name from the darkness a few houses down the street.

Watson and Ginger growled lightly at this sudden interloper and, to be polite to the other dog owner, I chastised them a bit, though in actuality I was happy to see my dogs coming together like a team for once. The man and I exchanged friendly greetings while the woman continued to yell the dog's name every few moments from the porch. I was thrilled to learn that the man had just moved back to his second-floor apartment with his wife. In my mind, two more people and one more dog under a roof within a single block of my house constituted a population boom.

We said goodnight and I continued up Palmyra Street with my dogs. I looked back over my shoulder to see my new neighbor and his dog heading home, toward the woman's voice still calling out in the darkness. Just ahead, I spotted another man sitting on a chair on the sidewalk with a newspaper held out at arm's length before him. He was middle aged and looked like he had been working outside all day, dressed in a dirty flannel coat, jeans, and boots. There was a brand-new white FEMA trailer across the street that I had never seen before, and a few yards past the trailer I noticed that the street was streaked with a great deal of running water. As I was considering the import of all this new stimuli along my normally lifeless dog-walking route, my ears picked up strange music coming from somewhere farther down the street. It was dramatic and formal and goofy all at once, and I couldn't orient from where it might be coming. I walked on, and the man sitting in the chair waved at me.

"Nice night for it," he called out agreeably as he waved.

"You back?" I asked, in what had grown to be the universal greeting for new faces.

"Yes and no," he said. "Back in town, sometimes back here. My buddy's got a place I'm sharing with him Uptown. You know, no power here yet, so . . ."

I followed the roll of his eyes back toward the darkened cottage behind him. Then I looked up to the newly restored streetlight shining above him and realized that he was sitting outside to read the newspaper because it was brighter outside than inside his blacked-out house. The strange music was still booming around us from somewhere.

"I thought that was your music," I said.

"Nope, that's them down there." He aimed his thumb down the street. "Marching tunes."

I listened more carefully, and I could pinpoint the source of music at the corner house down the block. It was coming from high up, though, like a broadcast pointed over the lower rooftops and over our heads with all its jolly, indistinct chanting, thumping tubas, and booming bass drums.

"Marching tunes?" I said to the guy holding the newspaper under the streetlight.

"German marching tunes. Strange, huh? I think those people just got back tonight. That trailer over there is new too. Haven't heard from them yet."

I continued walking up the street with the dogs, and we drew closer to the blacked-out house on the corner. It had a slim little balcony hanging off the second floor, and, while it was too dark to see for sure, it looked as though two people were sitting up there, their shadowy shapes rolling back and forth as if they were in rocking chairs. All the while, this strange, old-fashioned German music blared out of what I had to guess was a wind-up Victrola record player, which was emitting all kinds of mechanical clanking and the hiss and pop of old, old recordings between the oompah notes and drum crashes. The song drifted to its finish, and, in the silence while the shadow people up on the balcony prepared another record, I noticed the sound of something gurgling close by. It was the running water I had spotted before, and now I could see it was coming from a little spring bubbling up from a crack in the middle of the road pavement. It must have been a broken water main. The water was coursing down the street as a bona fide stream, or at least a creek. At any rate, it was big enough to fish in had it been running in the wild instead of down Palmyra Street.

Then, with a crash of drums and blast of old German brass, the music came back on again upstairs, pumping out its odd merriment to the neighborhood. The dogs were oblivious, lost as usual in the scent mosaic of the debris-strewn sidewalk and front yards. But I tugged them on and we headed back down the block the way we had come. I peered up again and saw that the two figures still seemed to be sitting there, rocking slowly on their dark balcony, while the antique voices of German women bellowed on from the old records. I passed by the curious new FEMA trailer again and came back to the man sitting in his metal chair under the streetlamp. He raised his eyes from his newspaper and nodded at me. He seemed to be reading my mind.

"It ain't normal," he said, chuckling, "but it's home."

Epilogue   The Unsinkable Crescent City
          August 12, 2007

Humans may be known in some circles as the tool-making animals, but two years after Hurricane Katrina roared in and treated
New Orleans to a municipal-scale version of the Poseidon Adven-
ture, I have begun to think that what really distinguishes our species is the ability to make routines.

Sure, a lot of beasts out there will go about their business day
after day in a certain pattern. But I'm convinced we are the only
ones who insist on imposing normal routines on situations that
are anything but normal, situations that might cause your average
caribou, for instance, to rethink the whole idea of the daily rounds.
When food dries up on a certain patch of tundra, I would expect such an animal to move on. When our New Orleans home
crusted over after Katrina, when our normally rich, colorful, decadent habitat turned into a forbidding and miserable wasteland, we
still woke up in the morning and looked for good chicory coffee, we still went to work, and we still hung out on our porches
at sunset, even if that sun was setting behind dead magnolia trees
and the scalped roofs of the neighbors' ruined houses. We still mark
our calendars for Mardi Gras, and even if we have to travel through
abandoned miles to get from our homes to a parade route we still
dress up in costumes and file in behind the brass bands when the
season signals that it is the correct time to do so.

But of course we still modify and adapt even as we go along
building and practicing our routines. At least once a week, for instance, I know just as well as the dogs that I owe them a trip to the
golf course. I have about as much interest in golf as the Amazing
Dr. Watson or Ginger, and that's probably the only reason I can bear
the state of the city's public golf courses during our regular trips to

155

City Park, a huge, beautiful preserve of green that stretches for some thirteen hundred acres.

Before the storm, a lot of those acres were occupied by golf courses. Looking at them two years after Katrina, you might not guess they were ever flooded from the levee failures, but you probably would not guess that they were ever golf courses either. The great oak and cypress trees from the original plan of the golf course survived, and the lagoons are still there, but with most of the park facilities damaged by the flood and most of its staff lost to poststorm funding shortages, the greens and fairways have reverted to nature. Overgrown now with weeds and mature brush, the vistas here between the patches of trees look completely foreign, like Brazilian pampas or South African plains. The only traces of human interference are the vestiges of concrete paths gradually slipping beneath the tide of green and the little golfer shelters here and there, looking now like burned-out African huts in a sad *National Geographic* spread.

Yet for the dogs, this is like Disneyland. As per their expectations now of our routine, I load them into the car every few days, drive them down a little service road cutting through the park, and let them out to romp. They tear through clumps of weeds taller than I am, chase water fowl from the marshy reeds of the lagoon into the air, and lounge under oak limbs that are bent and fused to the earth as gracefully as ruined Roman arches. We need no leashes here since the threat of cars lies acres away and there are no other people to be seen anywhere. These jaunts could only be better for the dogs if they fell upon a slop bucket of pizza crusts and beef bones in the weeded-out sand traps.

So one of our routines now involves running around this golfer's nightmare, while another one quickly became the daily survey of hope and agony represented by the real estate stock along Mid-City streets on the way to the golf course or just about anywhere else. On block after block, dazzlingly beautiful restorations of once-flooded historic homes brought back from the brink stand next to the disintegrating hulks of painted ladies left for dead.

It's a pattern all across New Orleans, whether presented so obviously as on the façades of houses or something wrapped up in our minds, leapfrogging among the emotions. The city is a quilt now of opportunity and desolation, stubborn optimism and darkest despair living right next to each other. People seem to switch from one to the other, torn by decisions somewhere between fight and flight or love and fear. It wears people out, and sometimes wears them right down. By the storm's first anniversary, after a year of the stress and loss and filth, four of my friends had shot themselves or fatally overdosed.

When we were stuck in Baton Rouge during the weeks after the flood, my friends and I hypothesized about what New Orleans would be like in the wake of the crisis, and I wondered what struggles and opportunities it would lay at our feet. That was after we knew we could eventually go home and after we had accepted the notion that normal would be a relative term. But it was still well before we really knew what we were in for. Trying to be reasonable, we never pictured the prolonged limbo.

All those months while I was wandering Mid-City in the dark, dreaming up metaphors for the tortured buildings and painting gas-light fantasies of bygone days in my head, the region's elected offi-cials and community leaders and various camps of engineers and consultants were making master recovery plans and holding hear-ings in giant ballrooms and meeting halls. Today, those plans are worth about as much as the reeking refrigerators that lined our streets after the flood. The plans broke down in strife, rejected out of hand by people who smelled a land grab plot in any suggestion of large, systemic change for the way the city's population is arrayed and protected. There is apparently another plan now, and even a new city hall executive in charge of recovery, though as closely as I fol-low the local news I still can't explain what it might be or point to any really impressive examples of civic achievement in the two years since the disaster.

But since life can't always wait for committees and processes, New Orleans has emerged in the void of active leadership as the ul-timate American do-it-yourself city. Residents are learning to take on the normal duties of municipal government themselves, band-ing together in neighborhood groups to map their community's future and reaching out to private sector organizations for erst-while municipal responsibilities. At the street level, literally, people have taken the initiative to erect their own street signs. Thousands of them were blown away by Katrina and washed around the city in the flood, and in lieu of much official response neighbors have painted their own colorful signs, reading "St. Philip" or "Solomon Place" or even "STOP" at the unregulated intersections and nailed them at the normal height on telephone poles. On the other end of the spectrum of private initiative, the public school system, widely reviled before the storm as criminally broken, has been joined by a dizzying variety and ever-growing number of privately run, publicly funded charter schools. Individuals have organized successful referendum campaigns to overturn wasteful or widely abused public policy standards, ending the election of tax assessors, for instance, and another citizens' group called Levees.org has been pushing Congress to hold the U.S. Army Corps of Engineers responsible for the levee failures that turned a hurricane into a catastrophe and to build more realistic defenses for the future. Progressive steps aren't coming from politicians and government agencies, but rather from enraged, determined New Orleans people planning and organizing around tables in their gutted homes.

Some days, it can be hard to find a parking spot on certain blocks in Mid-City among all the contractors' vans and trucks. The neighborhood can seem like one giant construction project, with so many heavy repair and renovation jobs going on so close together that the slap of nail guns, scream of table saws, and holler of workers all meld into one constant voice of active reconstruction. It's a voice that usually comes across in Spanish.

Taco trucks—the catering vans that specialize in delicious carnitas and barbacoa tacos with intense salsa for one or two dollars a hit—began arriving in New Orleans practically on the heels of the Red Cross, and they proved a harbinger for the tens of thousands of Latino people to show up here since the storm. Crews quickly arrived from Texas, Florida, Georgia, and the home countries, drawn by the obvious prospect of years and years of building work.

Now, when one looks down side streets off Canal, it's common to see young men playing soccer on the same blocks where before it was always curbside basketball games. The old, flood-damaged stadium at City Park that hosted local high school football is now home to ferociously contested fútbol on Sundays, the bleachers filled with guys guzzling Corona and singing unfamiliar fight songs. And at Finn McCool's, my neighborhood's freshly renovated Irish pub, business is just as strong when the satellite TV is showing a Mexican soccer game as it is during the England vs. Ireland rugby match. Even at the Palestinian grocery store down the street, a place specializing in pita bread, tahini, and halal meats, an aisle is now devoted to tortillas and black beans and canned tamales for the sudden surge in Latino people living and working all around it.

My house was repaired largely by a Salvadoran man named Joselito, a Mexican carpenter named Abel, and the six or eight guys who would arrive crammed into their car each morning. They've repaired a number of my neighbors' houses as well, moving right on down the block from job to job.

They are the face of the post-Katrina workforce to me, but Joselito and Abel were also unwilling participants in another trend—the rapid and brutal return of violent crime. Both men were robbed at gunpoint for their weekly cash payroll twice by the same gang, who seemed to regard these hardworking, Spanish-speaking people as walking, sweating ATMs.

The criminal slice of the population thrived here before Katrina, and it was the killings within their drug trade, people in their crossfire, and the occasional victim of a robbery gone wrong that helped the city post annual stats as the nation's murder capital more than a few times. Since the storm, though, criminals have had an especially free hand in the city, romping through its broken and ineffectual criminal justice system like Dr. Watson and Ginger roaring over the weeded-out golf course.

In the summer of 2006, when the mayor and the governor called back National Guard units to bolster the police department, I saw the surge in Humvees and military police on New Orleans streets again as a bad turn for the city's national image but also a welcome practical step to help make my neighborhood safer. There have since been mass community protests, a march on city hall, calls for the district attorney to resign, hearings and forums and consultants' reports. And, regardless, just about every day, a young black man or teenager is found shot to death near a shuttered housing project or in one of the drug-scarred neighborhoods, and people struggling to rebuild their homes and teach their children the beauty of New

Orleans are stalked by the fear of being robbed on the sidewalk for drug money.

After a particularly intense crime wave or news of some new bungling in high places or the impact of this or that new insurance rate or utility crisis, it's common to hear people around town declare, "I'm leaving." But I almost never hear anyone say, "I'm moving to New York" or "I'm leaving for Los Angeles" or anywhere else specific. They simply mean they've decided to leave New Orleans after one slap too many. But having cut that Gordian knot in their minds, they haven't actually figured out where to go, which is why a lot of people I know who say they're leaving don't actually end up going anywhere. Like a rocky, sometimes painful but still deeply rewarding and irreplaceable relationship, the city will hand you setbacks and frustrations that indeed make you want to pin a "Dear John" letter to the pillow and head for the door. But then you remember once again that you love the place too much to go, and come back from the brink, hoping maybe, just maybe, it will get better.

And it is getting better. Accompanying the do-it-yourself atmosphere here has been an eruption of civic activism, creative expression, and personal, carpe diem–style ambition as people try to wring something positive and meaningful from all the upheaval and tears.

The radio station WWOZ now features extremely contemporary blues songs penned about Katrina by local musicians. A number of my friends who lost or quit their prestorm jobs have started their own businesses. Erin Peacock, the one-time barroom manicurist at Pal's Lounge, now has her own salon, called Lux, while two other friends, Ian "the Other Ian" Schnoebelen and Laurie Casebonne, who had thought they would leave New Orleans forever, changed their minds quickly, opened a café called Iris, and soon won accolades of excellence from the national culinary press.

My neighbors in Mid-City, quite busy enough rebuilding their flooded homes and ravaged small businesses, decided during the first spring after the storm to organize a free music festival to show the rest of the city that our neighborhood was coming back. They dubbed it the Mid-City Bayou Boogaloo, produced it on a shoestring, employed dozens of musicians, artists, and craftspeople, and pulled off a major success. It's an annual event now, and in the spring of 2007 it expanded to two stages and brought thousands of people out to celebrate New Orleans life on the very spot where O'Brien and I had found that crashed helicopter and commandeered a skiff for my first journey back through the floodwaters.

In the Lower Ninth Ward, a nurse named Patricia Berryhill and the volunteer group Common Ground rebuilt her flood-wracked house into a five-room community health clinic, though from the outside it still looks exactly like the modest house where Patricia had raised her family. There are no traditional health care facilities functioning anywhere else nearby. Every week, the small staff sees hundreds of people, the poor and the elderly, expectant mothers, high school kids, people who haven't visited a doctor or nurse in years, and people who had robust health insurance plans before Hurricane Katrina swept away their jobs, all in rooms that were once Patricia's kitchen and her sons' bedrooms.

The big picture for the city remains depressing and hard to comprehend. Huge swaths of New Orleans are still utterly devastated, and the infrastructure of the city itself is in shambles. Two years after the storm, the latest estimates of the city's population peg it at about 60 percent of its prestorm level, or approximately 275,000 people living back within the city limits.

Threats and stress appear from every quarter, whether it's the sorry state of federal flood protection, Louisiana's coastal erosion crisis and its impact on our natural hurricane buffer, a dwindling corporate business sector, or the various scams and hustles to separate residents from their property and insurance funds, both of the homegrown and carpetbagging variety. Also, no one wants to get shot by a junior varsity car thief.

But I've learned that by tightening the focus, things look much better for New Orleans life, which, after all, never ceased being rewarding even when it was heartrending. I've learned to concentrate on relatively small issues and measure progress in the scale of block-by-block improvements rather than whole neighborhoods or anything like the whole region.

If my own block represented New Orleans, the city would be a comeback miracle. A few apartment houses remain flood damaged or in the throes of very slow, piecemeal renovation by their land-lords, but their lingering blight is nothing compared to the beautiful renovations all around them. Most of my neighbors have reinvested in their homes, and they look better than before the levee failures, with fresh, colorful paint jobs, updated mechanical systems, and in some cases careful historic restoration that has chipped away de-cades' worth of shoddy remodeling.

Many people here are striving to reconnect with the heart of New Orleans after its near-death experience. Joan and Al Arnold, a couple about my own parents' age, moved to my block during the first spring after the storm. The house where they had lived and raised their sons for more than thirty years in suburban New Or-leans East was annihilated by the flood, and instead of rebuilding there they used their insurance money to buy a shotgun across the street from my place. It was flood damaged, but they have renovated it into a postcard vision of sunny cottage living. In the early eve-nings, I often see Joan tending the flowerpots on her porch while Al plays one of his homemade woodwind instruments, which car-ries across the street with a sound like a mellow calliope in the gathering dusk.

All their possessions accumulated over decades of marriage and family life were ruined in the flood, but they seem to have adopted something like an existential attitude in the aftermath. I ran into Joan at Jazz Fest during the second spring after the storm when she was taking a few visitors around to see the sights in the craft tents. I asked if Al was at the festival too.

"Oh yeah, but he wanted to stay by the stage and watch our chairs," she said, referring to the cheap, folding canvas chairs that half the crowd seems to bring to the outdoor festival each year. "I think he's being a bit silly, though. I mean, my God, we lost every-thing we own in the flood, who cares if someone takes a couple of chairs?"

Despite the nickname of "the Big Easy"—a term invoked much more often by visiting sports broadcasters and TV producers than locals—making a life in New Orleans has never necessarily been easy. Even before the storm, it wasn't easy to find a good-paying job in the city's small professional sector. It wasn't easy to educate children with a public school system perpetually doddering on the brink of collapse. And it has never been easy to live in the path of hurricanes.

But people don't live in New Orleans because it is easy. They live here because they are incapable of living anywhere else in just the same way, and that's a big reason why people came back and continue to rebuild.

For those who care about New Orleans, living here has long meant living in a state of struggle and compromise, of yearning for improvement. That's because the city, with its irreplaceable heritage and tenacious culture, fulfills so many dreams and satisfies so many desires in a way nowhere else possibly could. But, at the same time, it leaves the most universal of American needs wanting—most of them economic and related to schools, jobs, and crime.

The people who care about New Orleans have always fought for it. They're the ones who battled drug dealers for the safety of our streets. They're the ones who fought to preserve the historic buildings and neighborhood fabric that give the city its character. These are the people who fought the uphill battles to make our schools better, bit by bit, to create jobs that can support families, and to assure that their neighbors had access to the most basic medical care.

Coming back to New Orleans after Katrina is not easy for anyone. For some people it will be impossible, no matter how much they love it. But I'm heartened to see that so many of the people who fought for New Orleans in the past are among the pioneers coming back and striving for their home once again.

As New Orleans emerges from Katrina, inevitably smaller, tougher, and maybe smarter than before, I hope the Big Easy nickname can finally be retired as obsolete. If we need a nickname, I'd endorse an older one—the Crescent City, an elegant tribute to the great bend in the Mississippi River that gave the port town its original form and purpose.

Better still, though, I'd prefer to update that old nickname for more recent history. For me, New Orleans will always be the Unsinkable Crescent City.